natural
superwoman

the survival guide for women who have too much to do

natural superwoman

ROSAMOND RICHARDSON

TED SMART

For Emily, with love

Acknowledgements and thanks to Dr Craig Benedict, Professor Alastair Compston, Professor Ian Robertson, Professor David Warburton, Dr Jon Kabat-Zinn, Andrew Turnbull, Julia Carmichael, Eve Brock, Jean Joice and Liz Hartley. Thanks too to all my yoga teachers over the years. Special thanks to my daughter Emily for her interest, comments and insights in many lively discussions during the writing of this book.

This edition produced for The Book People Ltd.
Hall Wood Avenue, Haydock, St Helens WA11 9UL

First published in Great Britain in 1999 by Kyle Cathie Ltd

ISBN 1 85613 714 7

Edited by Kirsten Abbott
Design by Kit Johnson
Production by Lorraine Baird & Sha Huxtable

A Cataloguing In Publication record for this title is available from the British Library.

Printed and bound in Singapore by Tien Wah Press

Contents

Introduction

The original concept of 'superwoman' arose out of the Feminine Mystique of the 1950s: she was all things to all people, she was the perfect coper, her life was perfectly organised, her home a model of perfection, she was a perfect cook, housewife, mother, partner, hostess and career woman. She was enough to give you a nervous breakdown. Times have changed, mercifully, and women's aspirations have changed with them. Women today who have too much to do, whether they be busy mothers, career women, working mothers or older women returning to work, still have to perform multiple roles. That much is not new. But what is new is how the empowerment of women in western societies has altered their consciousness. Perfectionism of that kind is seen for what it always was: ridiculous. The 'having it all' ethos of that vision of a good life has passed its sell-by date for many women who are evolving with new priorities, priorities which are increasingly grounded in ecological awareness.

The zeitgeist of the 21st century presupposes a way of living in balance with nature and leading an environmentally viable 'good life'. Natural means eco-friendly, it has to for our survival, living without unnecessary chemicals and additives in such basic areas of life as food, exercise, health, beauty care and home care.

Natural is essential for personal health just as much as for the survival of society as a whole, let alone the broader welfare of the planet. So 'natural', yes. But 'superwoman'? With all its connotations? The label requires – and receives – redefinition in this book. Women have a proverbial ability to perform multiple roles with ease, but their lives are often tainted with guilt when too much is expected of them and they fail to conform to an impossible archetype. This book restores a much needed balance, removing the stigma of perfectionism and restoring humour and humanity to a label which deserves to be used with respect. The new (natural) superwoman reclaims her right to herself and to her own life, without guilt, thereby enriching her input to her relationships, her work and to the community in which she lives.

What are the priorities of this new 'natural superwoman'? Above all, balance. To survive in a world that makes a kaleidoscope of demands on her, whose pace is frenetic and which offers unprecedented opportunities, she needs balance in as many areas of her life as possible – and certainly in herself. Busy women are reclaiming their natural inner needs in order to embrace the complex and fast-moving demands of the outer world: it is not a question for them of choosing between either one or the other, the inner and the outer, but of balancing them both. Somewhere out there there is a balance between home and work, family and friends, space and sociability, exercise and rest, eating and health so that a balance of mind and body, work and fun, masculine and feminine elements, right and left brain function lead to a life which is fully lived.

A natural superwoman takes responsibility for herself. She is intelligent about coping with all aspects of her life and abandoning guilt when she needs space and silence – that time to be which gives her headspace and the restitution that comes from solitude. This new superwoman is sensitive to the needs of her soul, awake to the doctrine of enough (you are not free until you know the meaning of 'more than enough') which prevents her from selling out to ambition or the false dictates of fashion.

This book prescribes no 'me-me' shallow creed of many new-age philosophies, but is, rather, a down-to-earth practical guide to achieving an all-important equilibrium between inner needs, material necessities, and interconnectedness with the community at large, so that life can be led harmoniously according to sound values which are universal to most cultures.

The new natural superwoman has to be a good time-manager, because balance entails organisation and focus. Which in turn entails intelligence. This woman knows that her brain is her best asset: Brain is Beautiful. By looking after the brain with the right food and right exercise, right sleep, and keeping stress levels down, she makes the most of her grey matter and has a better life as a result. Working with, rather than against, her body leads to a deeper understanding and awareness of it which can be nothing but good. This is the future for busy women. There is a terrible price to be paid for not looking after ourselves in terms of diet, exercise and stress: high cortisol levels caused by long-term stress cause brain-damage, indeed more than half of over-eighty-five year olds today have Alzheimer's Disease. We can avoid becoming one of that 50 per cent by looking after our brain-health. Health correlates with happiness. This is called 'grey-matter chic'.

Maybe all of this looks like a lot to take on board: but don't be put off by the prospect of what will turn out to be a rewarding journey. You can absorb what you need in your own time because this book is a manual for life, to use as you go along, incorporating what changes you can as you are ready for them, and to carry on using for different areas of your life over many years. Just select the parts that you want to do as opposed to what you feel you *ought* to do (no guilt allowed!) Empower yourself with those small changes that eventually add up to a new you. A little plus a little equals a lot; nothing plus nothing equals nothing. So even if it's recycling your household waste for the first time, or just doing a few minutes' stretching every morning or evening, or working with one particular area of stress in your life, the accumulated effect over months and years is substantial.

For natural superwoman is beyond age-ism. The innate wisdom of her understanding has nothing to do with years: it's about attitude, knowing that perfect is not a useful word, and that by looking after herself she will affect all areas of her life, enabling her to enjoy a fulfilled and balanced life – to the benefit of herself and those around her.

Women who have a good sense of humour and don't take themselves too seriously are not only more like to have happier lives, they are even shown to be more likely to succeed, whether in the world of home and family or the world of work. Pushy women are not always the ones who get to the top: very often it is the practical down to earth ones who get on with the job in hand, and who have a human balance to their lives, who don't even notice the glass ceiling.

A natural home

A natural feel

Your home is at the heart of your life. It is not just a base but a container for personal life and relationships, a refuge from the world with its noise, pollution, and constant demands: a sanctuary both for you and for others. When you unlock the front door at the end of a busy day you want to feel embraced and cosseted by the atmosphere of your home knowing that time is your own and that you don't need to cope with domestic chaos, an overflowing sink and last night's supper still on the hob.

Use of colour and light, sound and smell, flowers and plants, space and objects can transform four walls into a place, where order and harmony prevail, nurturing you on many levels.

The way you live in your house is an expression of your personality as well as your needs. You can bring these into balance by using natural, untreated materials in all areas of your home, creating an atmosphere of softness and beauty: they relax us, connect us to ourselves, make us feel good and restore inner balance.

Their uncontrived existence provides our link to nature when we are ensconced in urban dwellings. Natural materials give a soft edge to a hard world, offering relief from the relentless stresses of everyday life.

No longer the domain of the fanatic, eco-friendly is now a mainstream possibility, vital for health and, ultimately, survival. Our lives are surrounded and dominated by chemicals, pollutants and toxins which trigger health problems and endanger plant and animal ecology. Who wants them? The informed choices we make in terms of natural household goods, and recycling waste, are our individual chances to make a difference, both to society and to the welfare of the planet, even if we feel that they are tiny and insignificant. They all add up. And if you have children, the best example you can set is to bring them up in an ecologically friendly home.

There are more environmentally friendly items for the home than most of us imagine: furniture, fabrics, hardware materials and even clothes, are now made from natural materials without using toxic additives. Many of them are marketed through Fair Trade, and are based on sustainable sources and ethical principles. 'Eco-commerce' is the trade of

the future just as organic is the future of food. You can purchase with the added satisfaction of knowing that you are doing just a tiny bit for the ecological balance of the natural world, and that using your consumer power will help them to become more mainstream. A little plus a little equals a lot.

The global economy annually chalks up many billions of pounds worth of wasteful consumption, depleting natural resources and poisoning the world with toxic emissions. Responsible consumption and fair trade go ethically hand in hand, and we can all play a part in modifying, if not eliminating entirely, the detrimental impact of these forces on the natural world.

Becoming eco-friendly is so simple. This book will show you just how accessible it is and how small changes to your routine can have a long-reaching impact on your home and your environment.

It is becoming increasingly simple – and important – to use eco-friendly products in everyday life and to reduce unnatural substances in the home.

An eco-friendly home

Eco-friendly is not just important, it is vital. Literally. The eco-house of the future recycles waste bath and basin water to flush the toilets, uses solar energy and is insulated with recycled newsprint: but even if you're not going to build this eco-house, you can still use your consumer power to create a natural home.

Bathroom toiletries: toothbrushes, shaving gear, nailbrushes, soaps, toilet paper and body oils that have no chemicals added to them in their manufacture

IN THE BEDROOM

Organic, unbleached cotton and silk sheets, duvet covers, bedspreads etc.

Natural mattresses and wool blankets

Rugs coloured with vegetable dyes

IN THE BATHROOM

Organically-grown cotton towels, bath mats and bathrobes made with natural plant dyes

IN THE STUDY

Recycled stationery and printer paper

Flooring of sisal or hemp

Recycled cardboard paper bins

IN THE KITCHEN

Fast-boiling kettle to save energy

Ecologically-designed, energy-efficient refrigerators and freezers that use butane for coolant

Energy-efficient, low-water consuming washing machines and dishwashers

Recycled glass

Reclaimed terracotta tiles

Bamboo for just about everything! Flooring, tables, chairs, blinds, screens, cutlery handles, steamers, trays, baskets, boxes and mats. It is the most environmentally friendly wood on the planet, being fast-growing and easily replenished

IN THE LIVING ROOMS

Unbleached cotton for blinds and curtains, cushion covers and carpets using natural dyes and pigments

Batik vegetable-dyed throws over the chairs

Hand-loomed rugs dyed with plants and vegetables

Hemp and natural cotton rugs over coir (coconut matting) or sea-grass flooring

Rattan furniture or matting (it is a fast-growing vine)

Furniture made from reclaimed timbers such as ocean drift-wood

Raffia tablecloths

Lampshades hand-made from recycled paper and rags (very beautiful)

Green clean: natural eco-friendly tips

Creating an eco-friendly home is a conscious decision. You can start by not using aerosols: they are believed to damage the ozone layer which protects us from the harmful radiation of UV rays from the sun.

You can use organic paints which are made without harmful petrochemicals, using instead the natural plant solvents linseed oil and turpentine, natural resins, earth and mineral pigments and plant dyes. Not only do these come in beautiful colours, they are kinder to the ozone layer and they reduce the occurrence of allergies. You can even find floor polishes, wallpaper adhesive, household glues, varnishes and fillers that have been made without the addition of toxic chemicals.

Eco-thinking can even extend to your garden: along with using recycled waste as compost, use organic pest control in the garden (and in the house). Friends of the Earth and the Doubleday Institute both supply eco-friendly insect-killers. Recycling waste for the garden (food, fallen leaves, green and animal manure) creates diversity in the garden, avoids unnecessary chemical pollution and is easy on the pocket.

Recycle all your own household waste: put bottles, cans, paper etc. into the local recycling bins, and food trimmings on to your garden compost. You can buy tiered indoor bins for the different items to simplify this task.

See *Useful Addresses* on page 204.

ECOLOGICAL HOME ECONOMIES

Install solar panels

Buy low-energy light bulbs to save on electricity bills

Insulate the loft thoroughly with recycled newsprint

Lag your hot water cylinder to reduce heat loss. Insulate hot water pipes

Line your curtains heavily to insulate the room from the cold. Don't allow them to hang over radiators otherwise the heat goes straight back out of the window. Close the curtains at dusk

Line walls behind radiators with foil to reflect heat back and save on your heating bills

Double glaze windows

Line the grill pan with foil to reflect back heat as well as catch drips

Put draught-excluders along the bottom of your doors

Put shelves over radiators to deflect heat out into the room

Turn your thermostat down a little – and lower it when you go out. Use the timer wisely so that you are not constantly heating an empty house

Don't leave lights on in empty rooms, or heat empty rooms

Only boil the amount of water that you need in the kettle, making sure the element is covered

Mend dripping taps: you can lose one litre every ten minutes

Turn the tap off while brushing your teeth

One bath uses the same amount of water as five showers. Take showers instead

The virtues of recycling should never be underestimated. Use recycled paper for letters, envelopes, computer work, photocopying and notebooks. Use recycled loo-paper and kitchen paper.

A natural cleaning cupboard

When it comes to household cleaners we tend to want the best results in the least amount of time without thinking too much about the effect that they have on the environment. However, you don't have to believe everything the advertisements tell you: do look at the label to find out what's in the cleaner you are buying from the supermarket. There are many environmentally friendly products around.

It is now easy to find ecologically-friendly washing powder, washing-up liquid, cream cleaner, lavatory cleaner, fabric conditioner, wool-wash liquid, floor soap and heavy-duty hand cleaner. They are made from natural substances and are biodegradable. They do not contain enzymes, phosphates or bleaches and are not tested on animals, neither do they kill animal life in rivers and lakes after soaking away from your drains. You can encourage your supermarket to stock them by writing to them to suggest that they do: use your consumer power.

But you also can achieve the same sparkling cleanliness with only a few basic materials: soda bicarbonate, salt, lemons, glycerine, white vinegar and washing soda, for example, are just as effective as manufactured products. Remember that it's the soaking that has the most effect in removing dirt, not so-called 'biological action'. If you halve or even quarter the amount of powder you put in your washing and dish-washing machines, the wash will come out just as clean. Try it. Or use an eco-friendly laundry ball, available from Ecoballs, (see *Useful Addresses* on page 204).

Green clean: natural eco-friendly tips

REMOVING STAINS

Shoe polish stains on the carpet? Remove with white spirit and dab out remaining dye with methylated spirits

For ink stains on the carpet, cover with milk and scrub out. On the hands, use vinegar and salt

Tea and coffee stains on carpets? Spray with soda water, then sponge with borax solution

For beer stains, use soda bicarbonate to soak up the moisture, leave to dry and vacuum up

Red wine: put salt on to spilt red wine to soak up the stain

For tar stains, scrape off first, apply eucalyptus oil, then wash

For lipstick stains, rub in glycerine, leave one hour

Use soda bicarbonate as carpet shampoo: sprinkle on, leave half an hour then vacuum up

Saturate dried paint stains with linseed oil. Leave for a while, then wipe off

CLEANING

Clean natural leather upholstery with equal parts of boiled linseed oil, cooled, and vinegar

Use methylated spirits on a soft cloth to clean phones and computers, using a cotton wool bud for the less penetrable parts

Greasy marks on wallpaper can be removed by rubbing with a piece of bread

For limescale on plug holes: rub with a cut lemon

De-scale the shower-head in a bowl of warm neat vinegar. Use white vinegar to de-scale the kettle

For scorch-marks, mix borax and glycerine to a paste, apply for ten minutes, then sponge off. Or rub with glycerine

Use lemon juice or vinegar to bleach stains out of marble

Use soda bicarbonate and warm water to clean the insides of fridges and freezers

For candle-wax on carpets: cover with kitchen paper and use a medium iron to absorb the wax

Cigarette burns on the carpet? Rub with the edge of a silver coin

Sprinkle damp tea leaves on wood floors to help collect dust when sweeping or to keep the dust down when cleaning out the fireplace

Rub vegetable oil into dried paint on your hands, then wipe off

FOR SPARKLING SHINE

Clean chrome taps with flour to bring up a shine

Add vinegar to water in a plant spray bottle for cleaning windows – it cuts through grease and brings up a good shine. Wipe clean with newspaper – a cheap alternative to chamois leather and brings them up sparkling clean

For cloudy vases, mix a handful of salt with white vinegar, put inside and fill up with washing up liquid solution. Shake well and leave several hours

Use a spot of methylated spirits on cotton wool to shine up silver in a hurry

ELIMINATING ODOURS

A bowl of water in a room where people smoke diffuses the after-smell, or vinegar works well too and acts as a cleansing humidifier

Flush washing soda down the drain to stop foul smells

GENERAL HOME CARE

To raise indentations in pile carpets (table legs etc.) place an ice cube in the dent and leave to melt. Vacuum when dry

Keep wood ash from the open fire and use it to remove stains from metal and china

A fragrant home

The smell of beeswax polish as you come into a room, the drift of lavender oil from a bathroom, the aroma of fresh coffee and baking bread from the kitchen or the whiff of lily from a vase of flowers do much to create atmosphere and make your home a lovely place to be. They are even good for your health! It has recently been shown by researchers at ARISE (see page 85) that the immune-response is enhanced after experiencing pleasant smells. Beautiful aromas balance the emotions, whether their source be flowers and plants, pot-pourri, fresh herbs in a window box, scented candles or aromatherapy oils.

Burn these oils in a vaporiser, or use a room spray for the following effects:

UPLIFTING
rose, geranium, orange, lavender

INTIMATE
sandalwood, patchouli, jasmine

RELAXING
rose, neroli, lavender

CALMING
lavender, chamomile, clary sage

ENERGISING
rosemary, pine, lemon, orange

Flowers and plants

Indoor plants pour oxygen into the environment, and mop up excess carbon dioxide, keeping the atmosphere healthy. Keep them in the rooms you inhabit the most in the house to give you optimum energy. In summer, plant herbs in a window box to enjoy the aromas through an open window, and grow your own aloe vera in a pot to use for home remedies (see page 142). During the long dark months of winter, flowering bulbs bring light and pleasure to the house – daffodils, lilies, cyclamen, crocuses, tulips and hyacinths all lift the spirits with their beauty. A pot of jasmine is my unbeatable favourite, its pure white flowers pouring their scent into the house in the darkest weeks of the year. Gardenia comes a close second.

Cut flowers bring scent, life and colour to a room throughout the seasons of the year. If you add a teaspoon of salt, or a soluble aspirin, to the water in the vase they will last longer, so top up the water rather than change it.

Colour in the home

The ways in which we use colour in home decoration are usually more or less unconscious. Science has shown that the colour in our environment has a subtle but profound effect on us, both physically and psychologically. We can utilise the fruits of this fascinating research and become more conscious of how we live with colour. Complementary colours, opposite each other on the colour wheel, give the effect of perfect balance when juxtaposed since all the primary pigments are represented: red and green, blue and orange, yellow and violet. These polarities express yin and yang energies, broadly masculine and feminine.

Of the primary colours, red relates to the physical, blue to the intellect, and yellow to the emotions. Green, at the centre of the spectrum, relates to the balance between life and death: the chlorophyll that makes our earth green is in constant flux and renewal.

Certain generalisations can come in useful, for example, that a strong colour in the bedroom is not a good idea since it is not restful, whereas a tint, a soft and relatively pale colour, will induce restful sleep. Pure bright yellow will be too energetic to sleep in, pale blue-violet peaceful. Sea greens, blues and violets are wonderfully restful in the bathroom (see page 169), calming the nervous system and reducing stress. Pink is an intimate colour and supports positive feelings about the body, so is good in both bedroom and bathroom. White in the bathroom is clinical and uninviting, but wherever you do use it for its clean, clarifying effect, break it up with splashes of colour. Yellow in the kitchen encourages creativity in cooking, lightens the atmosphere and gives an optimistic feeling.

Touches of red and orange evoke hunger whereas blue suppresses it and quenches creative energy. Red is also good for conviviality so if your kitchen is the heart of your family and social life, use red tints. Don't paint the dining room yellow since it is too stimulating for digestion. For the sitting room it depends on what energy you wish to instil there: if it is a sanctuary, use soft blues and violets, if a meeting place go for the yellow end of the spectrum.

RED
Invigorating, vital and joyful, stimulating, warm, but a little goes a long way. For rooms of activity and alertness, for entertainment, amusement and celebration

ORANGE
Joyful and energetic, personal warmth, ambition, communicative, sociable. Wonderful for the playroom, dining room, kitchen and for where the young gather

PINK
The colour of flesh, loving, lustful, pleasure. A bedroom colour

BLUE
Calm, expansive, boosting imagination and creativity. Promotes relaxation, good for devotion, creating a spiritual contemplative atmosphere. A feeling of breathing out

YELLOW
Inner liveliness and stability, clear intelligence, detachment, can be ungrounding when too strong. The colour of wisdom and compassion in Buddhism

BLACK & GREY
Do not work well as paintwork because they have a negative effect. However, they may look good in touches, for example a black lacquer box, or pale grey curtains in a yellow room

Relating colours to rooms is highly individual and reflects much about our personalities.

These delineations give a general feeling of the effect of colour on the human psyche, but remember that the more negative ones can be used to beautiful effect to counterbalance the stronger, more yang colours: olive green with yellow, or dark grey with scarlet for example.

Feng Shui

Flowers, both natural and silk, play an important role in the doctrine of Feng Shui (pronounced foong shway). Feng Shui is a technique evolved by early Taoists in China, who believed that the energy of life force flows through everything. Where it is concentrated plants, animals and people flourish. Feng Shui affects your house, health, relationships, career, wealth and spiritual clarity. When you allow the full flow to reach you by skilfully applying its principles you get the maximum out of life. It affects your attitude to life, your energy and aspirations.

A house is full of energy: the positioning of furniture, appliances and mirrors can affect its flow. For example, soft lines rather than sharp angles allow energy to move easily. Plants have a radiant flow of life force energy, so placing them in 'dead' areas such as corners avoids stagnation of energy. Put them into your 'wealth corner' for prosperity.

Mirrors change the direction of energy-flow, so place them on either side of a long corridor to move energy from side to side to slow it down: hanging a mirror in the dining room reflects the prosperity and happiness of the table. Hide away your chopping knives in the kitchen, they cut through communication; and use a wooden chopping board and other wood elements for the kitchen. Throw away that angular headboard: it's for insomniacs. A light hung directly over the bed will turn you into a nervous wreck. So have a bedside lamp instead. Arrange your work-desk in a corner so that you sit with your back to a wall, and not too close to a window. Then buy a good book on Feng Shui, or have an expert consultation.

Living with light

Lighting can make or break the atmosphere in your home. Spirits are low in winter when the days are short, so try to get as much natural daylight as possible to ward off SAD: science now recognises the distressing symptoms of Seasonal Affective Disorder. Keep windows clean and curtains open to ensure you have a good source of light to read or work by, and use daylight bulbs. Low light levels make for gloom, and it has been shown that in dimly lit areas people become unsure and nervous, making for poor communication. Too much light on the other hand leads to general introversion: people close up, become shy and restrict their conversation. When thinking of lightshades, or even of coloured bulbs, be guided by the psychological effects that these can have, according to the language of colours (see pages 18-19).

Create a quiet space for yourself at home. My friend Mandy did this by painting a small spare room a beautiful blue, putting a futon on the floor, a stereo in the corner with a stack of favourite music – and a strong lock on the door...

File style

When I first set up house away from home I struggled with an inadequate plastic filing case which overflowed and never seemed to meet the three minute rule: if it takes longer than that to find, the system isn't working. Like many people, I detest inevitable paperwork and deplore spending time on it: but a proper filing cabinet is pure genius, it does the work for you. Each drawer is labelled with the compartment of life it contains, so even if you never read the stuff you know where it is.

Keeping a ring-binder Home Log Book is a flexible and long-term method of keeping abreast with running a home. Use it to log home maintenance and decorating, gardening ideas, quotes and costs, essential telephone numbers, a cleaning file to record useful tips and records of spring cleaning. List preserves for the larder shelf in the autumn, and Christmas ideas. Add your own ideas to this log.

Never throw away old address books – it's amazing how they come in useful.

WHAT TO FILE

The bureaucracy of life, for most of us, is about finance, insurance and important documents like passports, a will, contracts and so on. Allocate a drawer for each area according to your needs. Keep a drawer for receipts of expensive items so that if they go wrong you can get them repaired under guarantee (computers, clocks, electrical items etc.)

Another useful idea is to have a map of directions to your home printed and copied for visitors. Keep a file with an A–Z divider for other interesting things, such as places to eat, holidays and children's drawings and school work.

Whichever filing system you choose, clear labelling is crucial. Put tabs in front of the folders so that they can be easily accessed, and colour-code your files. For everyday areas that don't need to be filed immediately, use plastic folders or simple but indispensable paper-clips.

LIVE BY THE LIST

Making lists takes the stress out of home organisation by providing reminders and clarifying action. Treat your household chores like a job – which they are, albeit unpaid – and organise your home life much like you would life at the office, including setting aside a regular time to do the paperwork and correspondence.

Establish a cleaning routine so that housework doesn't pile up and remember that it is never finished. 'One never notices what has been done: one can only see what remains to be done', said Marie Curie. Just decide how much time you are going to give to it, and stick to it. When planning other tasks, allow extra time for delays and queues etc. so that you don't get stressed out.

Keep an annual checklist in your filofax or diary: car MOT due date, insurance renewals, membership renewals, checking direct debits, TV licence renewal, servicing of boilers, dishwasher, fridge, new road tax due etc.

Make a list of the important numbers that you need either frequently or in emergencies, and pin it up in a central position in the kitchen: it needs to include essentials such as doctor, dentist, vet, school/college, baby sitter, hospital, police, taxis, train information, plumber/handyman, cleaner plus any others that apply to your everyday life.

TIPS FOR AN ORGANISED HOME

Put out a pad in the kitchen or stick one to the fridge. Get everyone to write down items that need replacing as they run out

Jot things down as you think of them otherwise they get relegated to oblivion

Plan for pleasure as well as for work. Have a general outline weekend-plan – otherwise it can melt away

Insist that everybody in the family puts down their engagements on a central calendar

SHOPPING

Share the shopping with a friend: take turns

Plan to shop just once a week

Get food delivered, or bulk-buy. Shop by phone or internet

MAIL AND BILLS

Keep a supply of stylish postcards for one-liners or quick thank-yous

Keep non-urgent mail in a separate place from urgent mail

Get a set of small digital scales to weigh mail: it saves hours in the Post Office. Get their set of booklets giving costs per weight, and do it yourself

Bulk-buy stamps

Don't open your mail until you're ready to deal with it, even if that is tomorrow

Answer routine letters on the original letter, make a copy for your file and send original letter back

Put your regular bills onto direct debit and save time as well as bills being paid late

TELEVISION

Don't be a slave to the TV: set the VCR for your favourite programmes or films and watch them at a time that suits you. (Average time wasted in front of TV in the USA is four hours per day. Get a life)

TELEPHONE

Don't be a slave to the telephone. Let it ring, or let the answer-phone do its work

Bank by phone

Stand up when you're talking on the phone it gives your voice more energy

Keep pads and pencils handy for messages

Clear out the clutter

If there is one universal truth about home life it is that there is never enough room for everything that we accumulate. Getting rid of clutter at regular intervals is not only necessary to reclaim space, it is as energising as it is cathartic, and recycling is ecologically sound. The ancient tradition of Feng Shui is based on how energy flows through the house: clutter clogs your energy and slows you down. Get rid of it!

Do a 'user-audit' in the kitchen. Ask yourself if you really do need to keep that soda stream and when did you last use the pasta machine lurking at the back under the sink?

Hang your saucepans on a high-hanging rack instead of rummaging in cupboards for them. Keep cooking utensils in drawers by size, type and use, with one compartment for plastic, one for metal and one for plastic. Throw away duplicate can openers. Keep only the things that you use.

Clutter covers a multitude of sins: old clothes, broken toys, magazines, gadgets, paper clutter, old shoes and linen. Either it is fit only for the bin, or you can hold a car boot sale, junk-swop in the community (the Dutch put all their junk out in the front garden once a month, and neighbours take their pick!) or donate to charity shops. Recycle all your waste and simplify your life. Set yourself a time to do it, and do the worst first.

PHOTOGRAPHS

Keep photographs in albums, and keep them dated. You always think you'll remember but years later you won't… Throw out the duds and keep the negatives in their envelopes, clearly marked. Send spares to friends.

MAGAZINES

Rotate your subscriptions so that you are not inundated with reading matter. Pass magazines on to others when you have finished with them, but file any articles of particular interest before you do so.

BOOKS

I find it almost impossible to part with books, but if this isn't a problem for you then take the excess to a second-hand store, donate them to charity, or put them into the recycling bin.

CUPBOARDS

Turn out at least every two years and get rid of anything you haven't worn recently. For wardrobes, organise by length, colour, type (shirts, skirts, trousers). Use a shoe divider, and a shelf for hats and scarves. Make the best use of space by using double rods so that the longer stuff hangs at the back, the shorter at the front.

BATHROOM

Go through the cupboard regularly and throw out all medicines that are over one year old. Bin the rusty razors, those old hotel freebies, ancient bubblebath and bits of old soap.

CLUTTER CRITERIA:

Is it really useful?

Do I really love it?

Does it lift my energy when I look at it or think about it?

When you have decided, get four big boxes and level the ground: rout it, give it, toss it, or store it.

Simplify – have a long think about what else clutters up your life: too many diary commitments, too much furniture, inessential home equipment, boring TV programmes, unread daily newspapers, too many clothes and shoes.

The art of delegation

If both you and your partner have full time jobs, it really is unthinkable that the domain of household management should rest entirely with you. Quite apart from the fact that it will wear you to a frazzle, this is not a good example for women to set. How will male partners and children ever learn to co-operate if you do it all? Teaching responsibility to your kids at an early age is the best gift that you can give to the next generation (and especially to their partners). Sons who learn to do their bit will be less likely to dismiss chores as 'woman's work' later in life.

Don't allow yourself to become a victim of household chores. Nothing is less attractive than the smell of burning martyr. Abandon the outdated concept of the Perfect Woman.

Men have a point: the jobs are boring, tedious and hard work. Sensibly, they sit back and let you do it. I would if I were a man, I'd suddenly be looking very busy and important when it came to cleaning the oven. Get tough and train them. And if you catch them criticising the dust, hand them a duster.

Delegate within the family, and get help for jobs like cleaning windows, plumbing, gardening, dusting and DIY. This saves you ending up frustrated with a botched job and is well worth the money. Remember, there are people out there who actually enjoy ironing. If you feel you can't afford to pay someone to do it, swop with them for a 'chore' which you enjoy: weed their garden or do their shopping in return.

But there are certain things you can't pay other people to do, such as cooking, washing up, shopping and laundry, unless you employ some serious household help. Why should you feel guilty if you are unable to get these done every day in between running a job and having a life? Get your family members to 'share' rather than help: the latter implies supplication and puts you in a position of dependence. Establish a family meeting to prioritize the tasks that need doing, and allocate them by consensus. Make these meetings pleasant, over a favourite meal, a cup of coffee or a beer. Your partner may much prefer to do the weekly shop while you choose to clean the bathroom. With a young family suggest making chores competitive: who can clean their bedroom the fastest (quality-controlled of course.) Meet a week later for feedback, and make out a schedule for the next week. Clear, agreed routines save a lot of arguments: 20 per cent of marital rows are about who does what in the home.

MISTAKES WITH MALE PARTNERS

- **Thanking him for helping. Once you've agreed a routine, you are on equal terms, he is not 'helping', you are sharing**
- **Becoming impatient: however ham-fisted he is in the beginning with the vacuum cleaner or the saucepans, bite back the words. He'll learn**
- **Writing him off as a dead loss: 'He'll never be able to cook' are probably the words he is longing to hear you say**
- **Carrying on without sharing and resenting it with gritted teeth until the frustration erupts into a full blown row**
- **Not being clear about priorities: does he want to share his life with someone who is chronically irritable and exhausted and resentful, or cheerful relaxed and energetic? If sharing chores is at the core of this, then ask him to decide**

Establishing house rules and rotas is vital to maintain a collaborative and harmonious family environment. You aren't running a prison, but you can, with the right attitude, make this area of life run smoothly. Ask the family for their suggestions and co-operate with them just as you expect them to co-operate with you. Rotate the jobs regularly so that everyone has a fair deal. It's a great way to teach personal responsibility.

Being gently assertive about your needs will elicit respect from your family in the long run. You don't need to set yourself up as a monster of perfection: they will love you for who you are whether or not the souffle is perfect and the cushions plumped up. Encourage an open and understanding family atmosphere whose foundation is honest communication. Families need discipline as much as they need love, and a framework of rules not only prevents domestic chaos but also creates a harmonious home and a friendly, loving home.

SOME HOUSE RULES
No muddy boots beyond the back door; limits set on music decibels, noise-free zones either in terms of rooms or of times of day; TV-free zones.

Balancing relationships and work

Getting the balance

There has to be more to life than having no time to live. Women now outnumber men in the workplace but we are also, as ever, the driving force in the home and in relationships. Unsurprisingly, the latest statistics show that 90 per cent of women feel exhausted, and 42 per cent of these all the time. Work-related stress disorders are the fastest-growing medical problem in the western world. Surely there has to be more to emancipation than having too much to do? There is a balancing act to be achieved here; a balance between the demands of work, home, friends and social life, partner and family, and time for you (see Chapter 3).

One option for working parents could be to divide their professional lives into chunks over their lifetime: for example, 40 per cent of total hours when single or childless, 20 per cent when the children are young, then back to 40 per cent of total hours devoted to professional life when they are empty-nesters.

None of this is new: for decades women have coped with multiple roles. But what is different now is that, as western women have achieved a more equal status in the community and become more powerful economically, they can call the tune more than ever before. It is possible to have a successful career without sacrificing a sane and happy home life. It is no longer a question of choosing a job over a family but of finding ways in which these two can successfully coexist and complement each other.

This implies planning and organisation (see page 38), flexibility in the workplace, and not least the right ratio of pleasure and leisure in our lives. The key is to use time well (see page 36). Having it all is exhausting but it doesn't need to be. Plan ahead and always allow more time than you think you need. Realising you have no clean shirt on the morning of an important meeting gets the day off to a bad start, whereas a leisurely breakfast leaves you space in which to collect yourself, to breathe, to arrive prepared for the day ahead. Plan for household jobs, good childcare and home help and always build space into your day, allowing for the essential must-do's as well as personal time alone or with your partner or friends. Planning is paramount.

Women can pack a prodigious amount into a shorter working day before going on to fulfil their other roles at home in the family and community. The American Association for the Advancement of Science published findings in 1999 showing that part-time 'high-fliers' can get ahead faster because they accomplish more in a shorter time. Working fewer hours seems to be more effective for the upwardly mobile. As more flexible systems evolve, women (and men: men are parents too) will be able to combine successful careers with a happy homelife.

If you are lucky enough to work for open-minded and supportive bosses who understand and care, then getting family-friendly working arrangements is a great investment for him/her as well as for you: the stress of combining the two will lead to poor performance. In essence, the future of the workplace can only be successful in a part-time or flexitime culture, with a domestic democracy at home where 'the other half' is a meaningful epithet.

Maximum flexibility is the ideal. Systems-thinking (looking at whatever changes are needed within the overall structure of the company) looks for fundamental change rather than 'quick-fix' solutions, changing not merely the structure of working life but the attitudes that underlie it.

THE FUTURE OF THE WORKPLACE

Women now recognise their influence in the workplace and are calling for more accommodating structures which allow them to move in and out of employment without harming their careers.

In 1997 The Industrial Society published a survey of ten thousand young people under the title 2020 Vision. It was the largest study of its kind and what emerged from the aspirations of the young and up-and-coming generation was that the future looked female, focused, and flexible. Women, these young people all agreed, worked faster, could do several things at once and remain focused, could switch that focus easily and were better at getting along with people. Among their expectations of the workplace of the future were:

- Better communication with the bosses so that you have more say in how and/or when to perform tasks. Getting along with people as part of the moral climate of the workplace
- More than one third of them expected more childcare in the workplace in the next ten years, and to have more caring human-centred relationships at work
- One third of them expected more flexible hours to be available within the next ten years so as to be able to organise less rigid work hours for themselves
- Half of them thought that there would be more working from home. 'Women are driving the way we change at work' said one of them. 'It is all about flexibility in the workplace... We do the job in the end but it doesn't have to involve taking part in the faces game, just sitting at our desks and being there to be seen'

THE LEAPFROG PHENOMENON

Leapfrog is a UK market-research company which has attracted top female executive talent by pioneering family-friendly policies. It is run by two women and its employees have an almost unheard-of degree of autonomy: the children pop in, the MD takes her young son off to buy new trainers, the secretary's old dog snoozes under her desk and she takes him to the vet when necessary. One young P.A. organises her wedding and has fittings for her wedding dress without hassle, and if somebody can't take the pace and needs a day off they get it. Pregnancy and maternity leave are happily accommodated. Parents attend the school play, they are there at sports days, carol concerts, prize-giving and they can get home to let the plumber in.

Sounds pretty lax, doesn't it. But Leapfrog's turnover in 1997 was £2.1 million and attracted top clients such as Coca Cola, Saatchi and Saatchi, Tesco and ITV. They have proved that it is possible to have a home life concurrent with a work life. How? Everyone works in pairs (which differ for different projects) so that if the client rings there is always someone there who knows exactly what is going on. It is one person's job to co-ordinate everyone's diaries. There are regular staff meetings in the open-plan office and all details of all jobs are computerized. It is a close-knit company and everyone is familiar with each others' needs. The ethos of this company of like-minded people who understand each others' strains and strengths is to enjoy all aspects of life.

The guilt trap

'Guilt is petit bourgeois crap. You gotta do what you gotta do.' So says Woody Allen in *Bullets over Broadway*. Many working women, and women running a busy family life, fall into the time-honoured perfectionist trap of feeling guilty about failing to be all things to all people. The fantasy of 'the perfect woman' dies hard. According to research, 33 per cent of us carry a burden of guilt around with us as an accepted part of our lives. In the words of a working-woman-mother-wife-friend, 'You are what you are and you have to accept what you aren't.' She's brilliant at her job and a great mother but is a terrible cook and housekeeper. She has only just now, in her mid-forties, sloughed off the angst of her guilt by accepting herself as she is. Guilt is exhausting. Give it up.

Guilt can hijack your health, it is a stressor that makes us more vulnerable to illnesses and low morale (see page 69). Guilt distorts our choices and controls our behaviour and nothing is more stressful than not being in control of our lives. It manifests in insecurity, nervousness, panic and self-reproach. Who needs it? If the circumstances are making you feel guilty, change the circumstances.

Keep a positive attitude to your work. Allowing your enthusiasm full rein (remember the job-satisfaction, the sense of achievement, the fulfilment, the money...) will erode the guilt-driven habit of justifying or compensating. Abandon the concept of perfection and bring your roles of working woman, wife/partner and mother into balance.

Change the way you feel (guilty) by changing the way you think (I'll do *this* for a change). Our perception is our reality, so by changing one you change the other. The famous example of this is whether you see the glass half empty or half full. If your perception of a problem is negative, you will react differently from the way you would if you saw it in a positive light. So tranform your self-talk. Think flexible. And empower yourself by becoming more assertive.

Replace your usual way of thinking with a fresh outlook and make a habit of it. Neuroscience shows that anything repeated consistently for eighteen days creates a new memory-trace in the brain and effectively deletes old habit-memories. So change the vocabulary of your self-talk, avoiding the rigidity of 'I should...', 'I can't...' and the 'it always happens to me...' Lighten up. Learn to put things in perspective. See the funny side instead: humour is a great panacea.

The balance sheet

There is no calamity like not knowing what is enough
TAO TE CHING

Only you know what is causing pressure in your life and only you can decide what is necessary to fix it. Redefine for yourself in detail, on paper, the desired pace of your life, and your goals. How clear are you about your ultimate values? Are power and success in your career more or less important than a fulfilled home life? Are you prepared to make the trade-off? What is 'enough' as far as you are concerned? Side-step The Guilt Trap (see page 33) and make a list to cure the gridlock in your head.

Who does all the chores in your house? The writer and poet Anne Taylor-Brown said that every successful woman is in need of a good wife. Find a cleaner, farm out the ironing, get groceries delivered, buy in food for entertaining, get a gardener.

Ask yourself: are you organising your home life as efficiently and as happily as you run your professional life? (See Chapter 1.) Are your standards impossibly high? (See *The Approval Trap*, page 72. Let go of some of them.) Look at your work timetable and work out a job-share, flexitime, or arrange to spend some time working from home. Many people find that part-time or job-share is highly productive, you make better use of your time because you are more focused.

Weigh up all the options for child-care: is the current one working well for you? Persuade your bosses to start up a workplace scheme for child-care, or to introduce more flexible family-friendly policies, such as 'hot-desking', as the way forward for women in the workplace. Do it. Liz's partner Joe rearranged his accountancy job so that one day a week was carried out by a part-timer, giving him one day a week to share the child care.

How convinced are you that your organisation cannot accommodate your needs? Negative thinking may be undermining your progress.

Is it fewer hours, different work, less travel or just different hours that would relieve the pressure? Can you find another job that is less demanding and exhausting, but will also give you sufficient job-satisfaction? Can you find a job nearer home, to cut down on exhausting travelling?

SURVIVAL TECHNIQUES

- **Live by the list, a time-honoured stress-buster. The list helps to prioritise and also to keep to the priorities**
- **Delegate. Share the load!**
- **Learn to say NO**
- **Don't do it all. Work out what you want to do as opposed to what you have to do**
- **Go on a time-management course**
- **Take care of your health: take mini-breaks from work every ninety minutes, even just to stretch and breathe (see pages 96 and 116)**
- **Cut down your caffeine and alcohol levels if they are excessive (see Chapters 6 and 7). Learn to relax – even momentarily (see page 83)**
- **Check your regular guestimates on how long a job takes so that you're not always late picking the kids up from school: becoming time-sensitive is an essential skill**

In extremis, employ a company that gets things done for busy people, 'It's About Time' in California is a pioneering example. They organise your paperwork, sort out your cupboards, help with personal shopping, buy your travel and/or theatre tickets, buy gifts for clients, decorate the house, throw a cocktail party, pick up the shoes from the menders, organise house moves and just about anything you ask. (Or set up a business like this yourself and make a million bucks!)

Order out of chaos

For some women time management skills are innate, others have to train themselves: whichever applies, be pro-active and take responsibility for your use of time. Time management is fundamentally common sense: it's like looking at a map before you go on a journey, not after you get lost, or while you're driving. The benefits of well-managed time are immense. Gaining a feeling of control over your life is a big antidote to stress – one of the most draining elements in life. Time-management clarifies priorities and gives you a structure so that you to get the most out of life, both working and personal. It stops you from trying to do too much, and becoming anxious about the things that are undone. You end up with a life in which work and play complement rather than compete with each other.

Time doth flit, oh shit
DOROTHY PARKER

MAKE TIME
You can always make time, even if you think you never have enough of it. Once you have made time you can organise it better. The ballerina Beryl Grey said of the phenomenal Dame Ninette de Valois that 'she was a planner, and that's how she achieved what she did.' You can transform your relationship to time, to life, by ten to fifteen minutes careful planning each day.

This being said, you don't have to become a slave to organisation. Keep your mind open to new ideas and allow yourself to change course completely if necessary: planners are a guide not a strait-jacket. Some degree of planning is always useful as it will undoubtedly focus you more effectively than if you leave things to chance. (NB Don't do so much planning that you don't actually have time to get down to the things you are planning to do!)

ANALYSE YOUR TIME

It is important to analyse your time in order to work out if you are using it effectively and sensibly. Get a healthy balance in the working day and working week. Segment your day so that you have sufficient time for sleep, work and play. If you work eight hours and sleep eight hours, that leaves eight hours to play. Great! Planning these hours of non-work is vital, otherwise they get frittered away, or worse still get taken up by more work.

CLARIFY YOUR OBJECTIVES

Begin with the end in mind. Make a list of what you want to achieve, and by when, but making reasonable goals for yourself. The politician Mo Mowlam operates with three daily lists: work to be finished that day, work to be started (with its deadline) and a personal list for ringing the dentist or getting her watch mended.

PRIORITIZE

Prioritize your tasks. Be ruthless in pruning the inessentials so that you get things done how and when you want them done. Time-management helps you have a life. It enables you to spot the difference between the essential and the non-essential, the urgent and the less urgent. It helps you work out what you have to do as opposed to what you want to do, and to make time for the 'want-to's'. It means doing the essential work when your bodyclock is at its most efficient (see page 40), and doing the less-essentials while you are just ticking over.

FIND A BALANCE

Balance your time spent with friends or family and time on your own. Privacy is not a luxury, it is a very real need. Only with time alone do we gain perspective on our lives. Learn how to do nothing, too, it's creative. I have a Chinese proverb on my desk which says 'There is nothing that cannot be achieved by non-action'. Make sure that you block out at least half an hour to yourself every day: have a long bath (see page 169), take exercise, meditate, power snooze. Build in time to unwind, laze, daydream, indulge your favourite pastimes (see Chapter 3). The balance that you can create for yourself through time-management will bring serenity where before you felt anxiety about not managing to fit things in. No longer afflicted by the hurry-sickness engendered by time-stress, you will gain control over your life.

Planning and planners

Invest in a user-friendly planner, either a filofax, or a software package. Whichever you use, it is a tool to keep you focused on what you really want to get out of life, and to help you achieve that. It will give you flexibility and prevent over-scheduling with all the stress that results from the pressures of not having enough time.

Use the last fifteen minutes of a working day – or first thing in the morning if you are a morning person (see Human Biorhythms page 40) – to clear your desk and set it up for the next day. A clear desk makes for a clear mind.

Keep your planner useable, garbage-free, and handy so that you have it with you at all times. Essential contents of a good planner are:

A calendar so you can look at the shape of the coming year, make resolutions, rough out holidays, work projects and ideas, house maintenance, garden and pleasure projects, family commitments

Month at a view: so you can get organised for birthdays and anniversaries. No excuses for forgetting or not sending a card or present on time

Week at a view: an outline of work and play commitments, and exercise routines

Day at a view: a detailed timetable of tasks to do, calls to make, memos, exercise. As a general rule allow 60 per cent of the day for planned activities, and 40 per cent unplanned. Plan your day the evening before, allowing for the 'slack'

Contacts: keep home, business and work addresses, plus phone numbers, e-mail addresses, fax numbers, web-page details and any other essential information on these pages. Use A–Z dividers where necessary

Don't overload your planner like a bulging handbag but keep a section for taking notes of meetings, of phone calls and conversations, for making comments. Here you might also like to jot down your life goals, where you want to be in five or ten years time, people who have inspired you, or write down those elusive great thoughts as and when they occur to you. Plan for personal space and balance it against time spent with others.

PLANNING PRIORITIES

◆ **In general, double the time you think a job will take, to allow for delay, difficulty or unforeseen elements**

◆ **Allow a breathing space between meetings, appointments and commitments, to take the pressure off**

◆ **Don't spend too much time on any single activity – get the best from your brain by rotating tasks**

◆ **If things pile up impossibly, take the plunge and cancel a day's appointments. Create space for yourself**

◆ **Restore for yourself the blessing of time in which to do nothing**

◆ **Use pencil not pen in your planner so that you can easily make amendments**

Tuning into your body clock

Attention drops drastically after midnight: a bad time to drive home.

The ability to follow and understand your own natural rhythms and patterns over a day, a week – even a lifetime, will bring better balance into a busy life. Make the most of your highs and lows by getting to understand your circadian rhythms (Latin circa, around; diem day) which are monthly and seasonal too, rhythms of hormones, heartbeat, respiration and temperature, a powerful and inexorable timetable which dominates sleep, hunger, physical activity, mental alertness, mood and bodily function, affecting our performance at many levels, not just physical but emotional and intellectual as well. Our natural bodyclocks are triggered from the hypothalamus in response to light, and are genetically determined. These timings vary from person to person and the chart below offers a rough guide. It is possible to draw up an individual chart of your own unique biorhythms, so that you can pinpoint days when you may excel, or the opposite... (see *Bookshelf* page 204). Bodyclocks can vary by up to two hours – which is why some of us are larks and others are owls.

Human Biorhythms: a guide

6-7AM

Body temperature rises. The 'go-hormones' level rises. Sex hormones at highest level. Metabolic rate high: good time to eat a large breakfast.

10-11AM

At our most alert. Best time to use logic and learn new skills involving short-term memory.

12-1PM

Rock-bottom energy: body temperature and adrenaline dip. We are, it seems, designed for a lunch-time nap to recharge our batteries.

3PM

Body temperature and adrenaline rise again, while cortisol plateaus: ticking along physically and mentally, but relaxed and mellow. Best time for memorising and retaining long-term information.

5-7PM

Body temperature and adrenaline at their peak, muscles and joints stretched and warmed, co-ordination and stamina at their highest. Best time to exercise and use athletic skills.

9PM

The 'go-hormones' dip and melatonin levels rise - the hormone that relaxes us into sleep. A bad time to eat a large meal because metabolic rate is low.

11PM

Mini-hibernation – the systems slow down so we sleep without the need to eat or drink.

3-5AM

Body temperature and the 'go-hormones' slump to lowest level to allow deep sleep. Most one-vehicle road accidents happen at this time.

Humanising the work place

The ideal workplace should have (and a few do) a quiet room where you can take time out to reflect, read, absorb or just BE. But what if yours hasn't? If your job is a constant drain on your energy and you leave at the end of the day with your mind numb or still churning over you must teach yourself to let go. When you walk out the door it is over. Use the journey home as your personal space. Clear your mind for ten minutes using the mindful breathing (see page 200). This should allow you to shift gears between work and home.

If you can't humanise the workplace, at least you can humanise your home persona! The unrelenting pressure of a head teacher's job was stressing Jan out: after a twelve-hour day she would drive home like a zombie, bolt a glass of wine and collapse on the sofa. When she started to practise mindful breathing (see page 200) during the car journey it transformed her day, creating a mental space between work and home life and restoring balance.

Whatever the demands of the job, it's possible to make the workplace a less stressed place to be in. You can relieve tense or tired moments with treats: good coffee and tea (not slot-machine dishwater); the occasional cake to share around the office; a climate where it is possible to laugh and joke with colleagues; the ability to take a walk around the block or in the park just to get out from under, or to take a longer lunch break when things are not so busy.

If communication is good at all levels, it should be possible to negociate a fair and equal wage, a reasonable attitude to circumstances e.g. no breakfast meetings that coincide with the school bus or being able to get the washing machine fixed. You should be able to ask for a holiday or time off when you deserve it or when you choose, to say no to those repeated overtime demands with impunity, to ask for an overdue pay rise, child-friendly hours and to job-share (they are your legal right).

On a practical and aesthetic level, there is much that you can do to make a workplace pleasant to be in.

PLEASANT SURROUNDINGS

- **Keep (healthy!) plants in the office**
- **Have a vase of fresh cut flowers on your desk**
- **Keep personal photos on your desk, and hang pleasant pictures on the walls**
- **Aromas can transform an environment but not everyone's taste is the same. So keep them to yourself by having for example a bottle of coconut oil or a fragrant essential oil handy so that you can sniff it at will**
- **Make sure that there is proper ventilation so that fresh air flows in, and open the windows as often as you can**
- **Make the best use of natural light, or use full-spectrum light bulbs**
- **Adjust the heating and airconditioning so that the office is not too hot and stuffy**
- **Stand bowls of water around to keep the humidity up**
- **Use ionisers to counteract stuffiness and drowsiness**
- **Have the computer monitor at the right height (see page 93)**
- **Ration time spent using the VDU, and control the brightness**
- **Keep copy-machines in a side room**

Working from home

One problem about working from home is that people may not take you seriously: they think you can't possibly be working in the same way as someone who goes to the office. Friends and acquaintances drop in, invite you for cups of coffee, want to spend hours on the phone. Gently you have to disabuse the outside world of the idea that you spend your days on the sofa painting your nails. Gradually they will come to realise that your work time is sacrosanct and that something is actually being done behind that cosy front door.

Even though you're wired up to the world there are things you'll miss – the office banter and the company of colleagues. Business lunches become a thing of the past, so does dressing up – so beware of that all too comfortable old sweater...

Use sticky notes for marking projects, organisers and documents, and for phone messages and to-do ideas, but don't use them for filing because they fall off

With no clear demarcation between home and work, the two essential skills of time-management and self-discipline are paramount. You need to define your working hours clearly, and learn to change gear smoothly between work and domestic tasks. Finding the ignition button may take practice too. But learn to set boundaries around your working time and unplug for the weekend.

THE HOME OFFICE

Decide on a part of the house that is not on the main highway of domestic life (especially not the kitchen table) so that you can effectively separate home preoccupations from work and are least likely to be disturbed. Make sure it has plenty of natural light and good ventilation, and paint it the colour that suits your needs (see page 18) so that you want to work there.

Setting up the room for maximum efficiency involves logically thinking out how everything can have its space and is also easily accessible, in order of priorities. The ideal way to set up a desk is in a U-shape with projects (current and future) to one side, the computer, modem, phone and fax to the other. The central space is for you and your papers, organiser and in-and-out-trays. Keep nothing on top of the desk that is not in regular use – put photographs on a shelf nearby, and flowers or plants (good energizers, even artificial ones) on a separate surface. Keep your filing cabinets clutter free (see page 22) and easily accessible. Most importantly, get yourself an ergometric chair and measure the heights of your desk, monitor and keyboard before setting up (see page 93). Have good lighting for paperwork.

The maintenance of order in your home office is just as important as in an away-office. A lot of time is wasted on computers looking for lost files, so organise your hard disk, floppies and hard copy in a consistent fashion that is logical to you, and colour-code your floppies. Back up your files regularly – if not daily, at least once a week. Always keep spare supplies handy – nothing is more infuriating than running out of printer ink just when you are rushing to get a project off in the post.

Furnish the walls with a clock, a notice-board, and some inspirational artwork to give a sense of space and openness to the office. Hang some beautiful natural blinds or curtains, and burn some essential oils – basil stimulates a tired brain, rosemary aids concentration and both lemon and bergamot help efficiency.

There are crucial elements in any good relationship and all need to be nurtured be it with a friend, partner or family member.

How do these elements figure in your relationship?

Subsistence
Protection
Affection
Understanding
Participation
Identity
Idleness
Creativity
Freedom

Working with relationships

When it comes to juggling a work life with family relationships and friends, it's often the latter which take the strain. Harmonious relationships need constant surveillance and attention – and open communication even through the difficulties that stress, guilt and high expectations put on them. It is easy to fall into the trap of taking loved ones for granted if your energy is expended in the work place, but a mutually acceptable balance of give and take can be achieved if everyone's needs are openly expressed, with frankness, patience, honesty, self-awareness and consideration for the other.

Learning to read the male language of love and support is crucial in inter-gender relationships of any kind, whether with friends, lovers, in-laws, children or older people. A 'sociability gene' functions in women and not in men, according to research at Cambridge University and Wessex Regional Genetics Laboratory, so generally speaking, women communicate for relationships, rapport and sharing whereas men communicate for status and power. Women speak and hear a language of connection and intimacy, while men use and hear a language of hierarchy and independence, which accounts for how they often feel threatened by women's need to talk. Men are more likely to try to please through doing than talking: he may have put his heart and soul into that new fridge he bought for you.

Learning to appreciate the other's strengths, accepting them as complementary rather than compatible, learning to accept each other's limitations and concentrate on the good points about the relationship, are the most constructive ways of dealing with seeming impasses. See the impossibility of your high expectations: nobody could be all of that to another person. Accepting yourself as you are makes it easier to accept the other as they are, and to allow yourself to be loved, warts and all.

NURTURE THEM

- **Keep a birthday list in your organiser so that you don't forget important anniversaries**
- **Always have enough time when a friend or partner phones**
- **Call your loved ones even when you are inundated with work. Never be too busy for them**
- **Have a gift-drawer so that you always have a present handy. Send flowers when important things happen**
- **Keep a selection of favourite postcards to send to say thank-you for supper or congratulations on your great success...**
- **Keep making new friends as you go through life, following your instincts in picking them: we recognise friends rather than 'make' them**
- **Seek out friends from all walks of life, different age groups, ethnic groups and backgrounds**

Develop the art of being a good listener. And the even more important art of remembering what they've told you! (True attention is interest. The real art with people is to be genuinely interested.)

Be there for those friends or family in need. There will be give and take in any good friendship. Don't impose: be sensitive to their needs and they should reciprocate. Master the art of putting yourself in their shoes.

Communication skills

The starting point for any healthy relationship is learning how to argue. You may not want to bring up some point of contention for fear of being petty or jeopardizing the relationship, but suppressed feelings do not bode well for an open, mature relationship. Forgo spite and learn good conflict-management skills. Neutral territory is a good starting point: going for a walk to argue something out works wonders. Talk openly about individual concerns before they turn into major issues, and understand the huge impact of little cruelties, verbal or non-verbal (body-language is 70 per cent of the impact of a terrible row). One cutting phrase can undo many kindnesses. The Buddha said that expressing anger is like picking up a burning coal to throw at the other (it'll hurt you more than it hurts them). Self-control is the issue here, learning to 'ride the tiger' rather than allowing free rein to its destructive force. Use the energy and the strength of anger to clarify, to create new and positive directions, rather than to annihilate.

CHILDREN
Parenting is an untaught skill, we are all amateurs, however many books we read by erudite psychologists. Children instinctively know when their busy working mother feels guilty and have an artful way of playing on it. On the other hand if we martyr ourselves and give up our whole lives for them, they at some level resent the feeling that it is they who made us sacrifice ourselves. It's all about balance, and it's principally about love. Just keep on loving the monsters!

SOME TIPS FOR A GOOD ROW

- **Learn not to go on the offensive, or defensive, to get too emotional**
- **Stay calm, focused, logical, assertive, and good humoured**
- **Remain assertive about your own needs, yet try to understand the opposite point of view**
- **Say 'I feel', not 'You...' when accusing the other of something that angers you**
- **Watch and control your breathing: stay cool even when you are reaching boiling point. Breathe deeply before reacting**
- **Make requests in a way that encourages the other to co-operate with you**
- **Don't interrupt and don't get too flustered when someone interrupts you**
- **Give negative feedback in a positive way so as to avoid causing defensiveness**
- **Avoid sarcasm and spite. They can be satisfying in the heat of the moment but the hurtful memory of them will linger**

- Learn to respect the other: respectare is Latin for 'to look again'. Have another look, look more deeply
- Monitor body-language: use direct eye contact, don't raise your voice, avoid smiling to placate, keep your head straight and create your own space with expansive gestures
- Lock horns without taking it personally: a challenge does not mean lack of respect. If you have a good argument it will withstand a challenge
- Monitor your self-talk (see Chapter 4) 75 per cent of this is generally negative so reprogram to make it positive and self-supportive
- To keep the peace when a situation seems unbearably tense: say something sincere to the other at least once a day
- Learn to receive criticism, don't automatically reject it. Ask clarifying questions, be humble, and stay open-minded. Don't get hooked into defensiveness
- Bite your tongue when it is ready to lash
- Prioritize: is work getting in the way of nurturing your relationship? Have a lunch together to break the routine and maybe talk about it
- Find the fine balance between independence and inter-dependence, between individuation and a central alliance in your life
- See the relationship as a mirror: what you are confronting has triggered something in you which is being mirrored back by the other person. Learn from it

A STRESS-FREE SOCIAL LIFE

Don't mix with stressed friends when you need calm and quiet. Postpone the event tactfully.

Don't feel you have to go to gatherings you know you'll hate: get used to saying no nicely.

Don't bother to do things you don't feel like because they sound good and might impress people. Why?

Relax your standards and entertain casually: serve simple food and light a few candles rather than putting pressure on yourself with elaborate entertaining (see Stress-free Entertaining page 84).

Time for you

Time for you

Happiness is a rarer vocation than people suppose
SIMONE DE BEAUVOIR
The Prime of Life

In his inimitable film *Beyond the Clouds*, Antonioni has a character tell the story of people who walked so fast that they left their souls behind. This will resonate for many women who have too much to do. If you don't get enough time to yourself you fall apart: Time For You is a necessary investment because if you don't look after your own needs you will be in no state to be any good or of any use to others. Work, family and friends get the dregs of you, whereas if you restore yourself to yourself on a regular basis you will be more amicable to live and work with. Carving out time for yourself is often more of a problem than it should be. Either you feel guilty (the dreaded *Approval Trap* page 72) or under pressure: 'But I haven't got time'. Yet we all find time to do things that really matter. The crucial thing is to realise that Time For You matters. Lack of this time with yourself distances you, at some cost to yourself, from that 'inner power that is our inmost self' as Saul Bellow puts it.

The self-knowledge that comes from spending time with yourself recognises the power that you have to change and direct your own life for the better. We can, as we begin to know ourselves better, stop acting out unnecessary roles, challenge our assumptions, change habits, set limits, define boundaries, become more selective and learn to say no.

CHANGING HABITS

None of us are completely trapped by exterior circumstance, we only think we are. We all have a degree of choice about how we live in relation to each other and to society. Habit is mostly to blame for entrapment in wrong roles or places, and once you decide to change your habits – which takes courage, commitment and consistency – new doors will open up in your life. Look at it this way: an old habit is merely an established memory trace in the synapses of the brain: new (good) habits are fresh memory traces which commit us to a new goal. It takes only eighteen days to create a new memory trace to reverse patterns of thinking such as 'I don't deserve time for ME'. Time to yourself brings insights to see what you can change and what you can't, and the wisdom to act accordingly. And this may not takes years of intensive therapy… Trust fate.

It is clear that busy women have to create time for themselves in order to clear space for personal needs. So you may need to be more assertive than you are used to being. You may need to look very specifically at the things you can do to change your internal resistance to 'me-time' – which may mean altering your home environment, routines, diet, leisure interests or even just your personal appearance. It may be that you find it difficult to stop running, to stand still, to be with yourself, to take a walk, to read a book, to pursue a favourite hobby or just treat yourself to some bodywork. Or just to do nothing. Even if it is only snatching a few precious minutes between commitments, to breathe, to relax, to undo the mental and physical tensions that assail you, you will find some respite, some relief.

LETTING GO

It's surprising how hard some of us find it is to be nice to ourselves, to let go of the negatives implanted by our self-talk (and by others) and face up to the possibility that we are addicted to The Approval Trap, of caring too much what people think or what they might say, worrying about rejection and perpetuating the habit of feeling guilty. Don't buy into this negativity. I learnt a great 'letting-go' lesson on a horse: I was terrified of learning to canter, it seemed so fast and dangerous, and everything was getting in a muddle because I was rigid with tension. The poor horse couldn't understand the instruction to canter while at the same time my body was saying 'Stop! I'm so scared!' I finally became so desperate at my incompetence that I said to myself, 'I don't care!' – whether I fell off or whether I couldn't stop the horse (we were only in the riding school) – I just didn't care. I hurled myself into the hands of Fate. I relaxed... We immediately went into the most perfect, easy-going canter. It was a life lesson for me.

It is not wise to rush about... If too much energy is used, exhaustion will follow
LAO TZU
Tao Te Ching

DO IT

- **Say 'I don't care' to yourself**
- **Take off your watch**
- **Relax, let go of the 'ought-to's' and create your own soul time, one step at a time**
- **Be positive, and be easy on yourself**
- **Don't agonise, don't procrastinate (you are not alone, we all do that)**
- **Prioritize, and schedule some Time For You into your busy life. Now. Today**
- **Forgive and forget: let go of grudges. *Ex* means out – forgiveness removes them from your orbit**

The therapy trap

Therapy means healing. 'Psyche' (literally 'breath') is the ancient Greek for 'soul' and 'spirit.' Psychotherapy means healing the soul. A good therapist will intuitively work with this in view, creating a safe, neutral space in which her client can reconnect with her soul needs. But certain therapists have moved from this transpersonal definition towards an analysis-based, self-affirming resignation which makes outdated excuses rooted in blaming others for past mistakes. How unattractive this intense self-absorption. It's a nasty vice to blame your life on your parents (imagine being a ninety-year old and still furious about your potty-training). Adapting to the perceived injustices of existence by replacing shame with blame, a pacifying escape from the 'sea of troubles' we all suffer, represents an excuse not to take responsibility for our adult life. Even the famously ex-psychotherapist Alice Miller finally came to the conclusion, after several best-selling books on analysis, that 'maybe it is not so important to look back in order to find a way to organise one's life in the present.'

THE TALKING CURE

Getting things off your chest (the 'talking cure') is known – has always been recognised – to be a powerful panacea, and although people in deep trouble need serious help, for most of us, a handful of sessions with a good counsellor (the value of cognitive therapy is indisputable), or unburdening to a sympathetic listener (and being able to hear their problems, too, if necessary), or sharing confidences in a high-quality environment such as a well-facilitated group, will free us up and do a lot for happiness. Such self-disclosures undoubtedly help clarify our minds, gain insights and grow out of our problems. They soothe emotional turmoil and improve our psychological state, they even improve immune function and physical health. A little therapy may be a route to salvation but it is not the salvation itself. Personal responsibility is that salvation.

There is all the difference in the world between those independent processes and the intrusive probings towards the self-revelation of another, invasive analysis grounded on a polarised dependence which creates a trap from which it is difficult to extract oneself intact. It can be as addictive as any drug. And there is little evidence of its efficacy, or that it changes anything much for the better in the long-term, or that it reconnects the client to a living sense of community, social environment and the needs of others.

BEWARE THE QUICK FIX!

The unfocused 'spirituality' of New Age psychologies doesn't much help us take

*Learning to be,
to be still,
to do nothing,
to enjoy silence
and solitude
presupposes
letting go
of the many
strings that
attach us
like puppets
to the
extraneous.
Watch the
stars,
smell the
honeysuckle,
listen to
the birds,
feel the grass
under your feet,
touch the
velvety petals of
a rose.*

Creativity cures the chaos in the heart
TIBETAN PROVERB

up arms against 'outrageous fortune' either. These narcissistic, intellectually vapid eclectic quick-fixes induce shallow touchy-feely responses and an ignorant conviction of finding answers to the eternal mysteries. They, along with much of the contemporary culture of analysis, nurture self-love above self-knowledge and selfishness above selflessness. They insist on re-forming us according to their doctrines rather than allowing us to become truly ourselves. The cleverness of 'knowing' through introspection (though merely through the particular lens of the dogma) confuses knowledge with understanding and experience.

SHRINKING THE PSYCHE

The analyst – significantly known as the 'shrink' – cannot by this definition embrace the completeness and complexity of our multiplicity. Nearly a century of deconstructive psychoanalysis does not appear to have reawakened the collective soul to the rich cosmology of the psyche so familiar to the poets and religious mystics of the past. Rather, it seems to have colluded with society's tendency to de-sensitize, to secularize, and to blame. It fails to preserve the sense of open possibilities that would connect it so powerfully with perennial philosophies, it fails to help us become more alive, more awake. It shrinks, indeed, the potential of the psyche to open: as Jung pointed out more than once, psychotherapy needs to relocate the patient within the psyche, not assume that the psyche is stuffed inside the patient.

THE ABUSE OF POWER

The therapist-client relationship invites abuse of power. Clients often approach the therapist as a surrogate priest or parent, which may for a time have a healing effect but which runs the risk of projective identification and the loss of autonomy. Judgement and critical faculty become impaired by a confessionalism which creates a one-sided vulnerability, and clients become the target of an exploitation of power whether knowingly or not. Many millions of dollars are made by the therapist on the counselling couch, although there are of course good and bad therapists. At best, the therapist-client relationship can be illuminating, healing, nurturing and creative, and enable better intimate relationships and more meaningful lives in the world. At worst it is manipulative, undermining and destructive, and very expensive. Many are the victims of the analytical-therapy trap which locks the client into a dependency from which there is no clean escape: because the therapist will always have the last word. There is even a school of thought that psychotherapy is the thinking person's equivalent of pornography where people pay to emotionally strip for strangers at expensive therapy sessions tantamount to voyeurism.

TAKING RESPONSIBILITY

I was lucky: I found a wise woman who clarified much for me at a time when I needed guidance, who untied some internal tangles with me, and who set me up to continue my life journey better equipped than before. I emerged from my few sessions with her with stronger foundations of self-esteem and knowledge about who I am, yet grounded in the ethical philosophy and spirituality that have always been core to my view on life. But many are not so lucky.

In the end women have to take responsibility for their own lives and happiness, and there are ways of doing this that do not have to depend on the expensive and potentially abusive intervention of others. Most of us need help, guidance, support and clarification along the way, and though you may find elements of this in professional counselling, it is just as likely that you will find it in sharing with good friends, reading wise texts (books are often our guides), in mindfulness meditation practice (see page 200) and in other non-verbal activities such as listening to music, or communing with nature. To enable you to do this, you need time for yourself.

To schedule Time for Yourself into a busy life you need to be clear about what you have to do as opposed to what you think you ought to do. So make a list of each, and weed out the unnecessary 'ought-to's'. Knowing what you are good at and doing it is just as important as knowing what you are not good at and either avoiding it or delegating. The same applies to what you want to do with your life, and what you do not want to do with your life.

SAY 'YES' TO YOURSELF

For this to happen, you may well need to undo some of your conditioning. You can break habits of a lifetime and cease living in the land of 'ought to be', both in regard to yourself and also in the realm of your expectations of others.

Rather than seeing a shrink in your spare time and relinquishing your power to an external authority, carve out your own space to do the things that matter to your soul. You are more likely to open up to life and its possibilities and to find peace and self-knowledge. To find an opening one has to make a breach in the wall – and the wall is almost always in one's own mind. The psychologist Abraham Maslow wrote that people who

What progress have you made if you have neglected yourself?
Thomas à Kempis
(15th century Augustinian monk)

are happy with themselves find it easier to be happy with, and give love to, other people. If we are not in good shape, how can we be of use to anyone else? Time for you redresses the balance between life's demands and your inner resources. It is a truly good investment, it recharges your soul batteries and replenishes your energy to deal with the demands made on you. Learn to say 'no' to other people and 'yes' to yourself for a change. Without guilt.

Julia's test

Many years ago I took myself off to see a counsellor called Julia who helped me untangle some of the knots in my mind. She perceived that I was not particularly good at being nice to myself (at the time – I am now, thanks to her test). She told me to go off and spend £100 on myself. I gasped inwardly and thought 'I can't possibly do that'. But as the days passed I began to think, 'What if I had £100, what would I buy for myself that I really want, or need, or which would give me pleasure?' One morning I went shopping and spent my £100, all in one go as she had recommended. I have never forgotten the experience and the effect has stayed with me. Try it. You're worth it.

Reward yourself

So you have built in your time for you. What are you going to do with it? The answer is uniquely personal. Where one person may find restoration in solitude, the next person needs a gossip and a laugh with friends. The important thing is to recognise what works for you. Personally I love being alone, but conversely I also love talking over a meal with wine and friends. I love messing about with my dog, talking to my cat and wandering around the countryside on a horse. For all my lifestyle I love – to many people's surprise – Grand Prix racing. Totally unecological, male-dominated and disastrously expensive as it is, nobody and nothing is allowed to disturb me on the sofa where I am to be found for every race. 'You will do foolish things', wrote Colette, 'but do them with enthusiasm.' My daughter, who lives in the city, will dive into a gallery and gaze at a Rothko painting for half an hour, or go to an early evening movie, emerging refreshed and revived for the rest of the day.

Your best friend is yourself
BOETHIUS

Break your routine completely. Do something unconventional (it improves brain function, according to research).

Do your thing, and don't be tempted to spend your Me-Time doing things you don't want to do just because you think you ought to. I love comedy programmes on TV, Irish music in Irish pubs, playing classical music at home, loud, and going to the cinema. I indulge these activities in between the demands made on me by a working life and running a home. 'The practice is primary', said the great philosopher Wittgenstein. The important thing is to do it.

There are many simple and inexpensive ways to escape from the worries and pressures of everyday life. See if a few of them work for you. When they do, they can have an effect that may last for days. According to ARISE, Associates for Research into the Science of Enjoyment, only ten minutes after listening to a favourite piece of music a saliva test shows that higher levels of disease-fighting antibodies are activated in the body. So your Time for You is also your best medicine.

Most of us feel guilty when we allow ourselves to have a nice time. Give up this kind of guilt: it is a negative energy. See the positive side and call it 'self-altruism'. By looking after yourself you will be better able to be nice to others. Be 'self-ish' in order to be unselfish.

SWEET TREATS

- **Get lost in a novel or a film**
- **Start a new learning curve: learn a new language, teach yourself chess, join a creative course**
- **Daydream, fantasize. Sometimes dreams come true**
- **Have an aromatic bath. Book a facial or a massage. Redefine yourself with a new hairdo**
- **Revamp your wardrobe**

Buy or pick some flowers and put them in a place where you work – the kitchen, the study – not just the living room

- Play tennis, go swimming, cycling, running, walking
- Leave the ironing, ignore the shopping list and don't look at the dust, and go and do what you enjoy doing
- Dance till you drop
- Indulge little rituals that you enjoy: a cappuccino in a favourite cafe
- Develop the senses: look at great paintings or beautiful trees; smell lilies; listen to music; stroke a cat; savour the flavour of a delicious meal
- Go and sit by a river, or by the sea. Gaze at the water
- Do something creative like painting, knitting, gardening, singing, drawing, sewing or writing a poem
- Take yourself off to an exhibition or a lecture, have lunch in a new place, go to the theatre, the opera or ballet
- Stay in the present moment and appreciate it: keep the 'immortal demons of futurity' (William Blake) at bay
- Stargaze

Make a list of role-models of the women you either know personally or have admired, who have never stopped learning and who are as a consequence young at heart and mind, like Nancy, below.

MAKE THE MOST OF YOUR MIND

Self-esteem is reinforced by spending time in activities that you enjoy, so Time for You is part and parcel of survival in a world which makes intense demands on you. Taking care of diet (see Chapter 6), health (see Chapter 7) and taking natural exercise (see Chapter 5) are intrinsic to good self-esteem too. But perhaps above all, although inseparable, making the most of our minds empowers us. By continuing to educate yourself and fulfilling your creative side, you stop brain cells dying of boredom which they otherwise do. 'Use it or lose it' has been proved by neuroscientists to be an infallible truth.

Self-esteem is strengthened by the absorbing processes of learning and creative expression. The synaptic connections in your brain grow and actually physically improve their powers of association if you present constant fresh challenges to your thinking apparatus. The more you learn, the easier it becomes. The brain is a slumbering giantess: according to the latest brain research we use only one per cent of its potential capacity! Leonardo da Vinci exhorted us to study the science of art, and the art of science, to develop our senses and to learn how to see. To do this we need to develop right brain function (rhythm, dimension, colour, imagination, day dreaming, and spatial relationship) as much as left brain function (logic, learning, number, sequence, analysis and listing).

Training your mind is a form of aerobics for the brain. Those grey cells are your greatest asset and you do well to use them to their fullest potential. Otherwise you will end up with an unlived life, a life which on looking back was full of work and chores and 'ought-to's'.

LEARNING TO LIVE

'The aim of life', says Henry Miller, 'is to live, and to live means to be aware, joyously, serenely, divinely aware.' Developing a positive, confident attitude to the possibilities and changes that life presents is within the capability of all of us, and Time for You accommodates this flexibility. Learning to give yourself a break, to play, takes practice. But nothing happens until we take responsibility, and decide that we are more than who we have learned to be. And the rewards are incalculable. Our lives are of our own making and it is down to us to decide the outcome.

The power of music

There is evidence that listening to music has surprising physical and mental effects: classical music such as Bach can help you solve academic problems, and certain music has been shown to improve concentration and facilitate learning in children. Some clinics play Mozart to women in childbirth and report easier labour and delivery. Music can lower the pulse rate, body temperature and heart-rate. It has been shown that calming music leads to altruistic behaviour (and conversely aggressive music leads to aggressive behaviour.) Above all, music – when it is not of the aggressive, profane kind – has been shown to reduce stress levels. Cheaper than Prozac, ecologically sound, and no side effects.

THE FOURTH DIMENSION

Work and the demands of family life, of relationships and community, are means to an end. Play, however, is an end in itself. We can afford not to be in deadly earnest, but to allow ourselves to be at home with ourselves with an activity that has intrinsic value to us. By this we are inwardly restored to the exhilaration and innocence of childhood, and nowhere is this more apparent than in the realm of music, the structures of which reflect the life of the soul. Aristotle said that 'when we listen to such representations (rhythms and melodies) we change in our soul'. Music is the fourth dimension, its spirit is free from concepts and thus it is the universal idiom that can be understood by us all. Its non-verbal

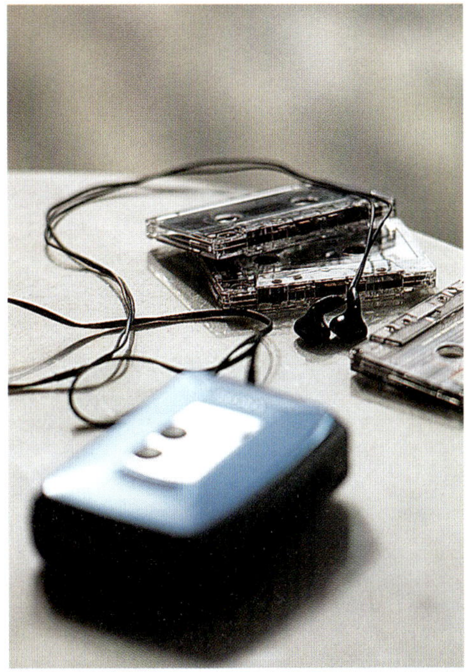

power reaches the soul, and at its greatest can have a profound effect that only religious language can describe.

The art of music was represented by the ancient Greeks by the lyre of Apollo which symbolises the transcendent nature of music. There is music that soothes, that uplifts, that moves the heart deeply, that elucidates and clarifies, that transports. Music is food and drink for the soul: it nourishes the psyche, and slakes its thirst for the transpersonal and the non-verbal. It is a mirror of our understanding. If harmony is the language of human feeling, then melody is the experience of relationship and character, and rhythm the pulse of life. Its metaphors feed our imagination and replenish the soul. We reach out of ourselves through music: this is true therapy in its original meaning of healing.

Surviving stress

What is stress?

Stress is a fact of life, but there is 'good' stress and 'bad' stress. Good stress can be exciting and motivating – a quick adrenalin rush which charges you up. Bad stress happens when the demands made on you exceed your capacity to cope with them, and overwhelm you. How stress affects you depends on how you respond to a situation. Attitude is all. Attitudes demonstrate the extent to which our lives are influenced by the way we think. It's not merely that the things that happen to us are stressful, it is our perception of events and the way we react to them that determine stress levels. It is within our power to control our responses by monitoring our thoughts and deciding on a positive attitude.

EARLY WARNING SIGNS

◆ Are you tired all the time? (Parents at Work Organisation have found that 72 per cent of working mothers say they are.)

◆ Are you often irritable and short-tempered with your nearest and dearest?

◆ Does a tight deadline exhilarate or depress you?

◆ Do you have weekend headaches and recurrent colds and coughs?

◆ Do you sleep badly?

◆ Is the only way to defuse after a hard day at the office a cigarette or a glass of wine?

◆ How much alcohol do you *really* drink when you get home from work?

◆ Do you raid the fridge for consolation? Are you over-eating?

◆ Is your self-talk mostly negative? 'It's no use', 'He/she is getting me down', 'I can't...'

When researching this book I went to a 'stress solutions' day seminar about forty-five minutes' drive away. Settling down with my breakfast that morning I started to read the notes I'd had no time to look at. 'Be there promptly by 9 a.m...' My watch said 8.10. No make-up on, teeth unbrushed, and only one gulp of coffee into the day, I flew. Five minutes into the journey the road was blocked where a lorry had crashed. No hope of squeezing past. The only possible detour would add six miles to my journey. I was going to be late. Being late stresses me, and I was already stressed. I turned the car around to take the alternative route, tyres screeching, shoulders tense, railing at my misfortune. Then I thought: which is better, late or dead? Late. By now it was inevitable. I slowed down. I decided to enjoy the drive through the May countryside, all cow parsley and hawthorn blossom, to breathe, to calm myself and to recognise that it did not matter that much if I was not on time. I arrived, much to my surprise, with one minute to spare. And the opening sentence was about how human beings can alter their lives by altering their attitudes of mind!

Stress gets you going. Without it we would all be very 'nice' and boring (probably bored too). Depending on your reaction to it, stress can give you positive energy from a healthy adrenalin rush, aiding creativity and performance. Mild stress is even physically good for you, having widespread beneficial effects on immune function. Short-term stress is exhilarating: some people thrive on it. It gives you that boost you need for challenges, such as when you meet the boss for lunch to discuss your latest project or a pay rise. 'Good' stress is what you make of it, you can make it work for you by using it to trigger change, learning and growth.

Chronic stress, however, has a uniformly negative effect: it is a form of distress which, in the long term, damages both body and brain (see *The Stress Response* page 69).

THE COST OF STRESS

Stress is a clear message to change something in our lives – for the better. It is the disease of the late 20th century, one that we are all too familiar with. Stress-related illnesses are costing the industrialised world billions of pounds each year (representing a significant percentage of the the GNP in both the USA and UK). Of premature deaths, over half are related to stress: coronary heart disease being the main killer. We literally work ourselves to death. Is it worth it?

As stress levels rise the medical profession is attempting to reduce them by prescribing sleeping pills, anti-depressants and tranquillizers. There are however natural solutions (see Chapter 7) which do not have side effects, nor do they lead to dependency or addiction. Popping pills does not address the core problem, it merely relieves the symptoms. Drugs that reduce anxiety also reduce vigilance, reaction-speeds and efficiency. As you increase the dosage you become less in touch with your real feelings. Drugs are not a long-term solution, nor are habits such as alcohol, smoking and comfort-eating. Although we cannot avoid the stress factors of today's world, we can use techniques to cope with them.

TAKE RESPONSIBILITY

Busy women who want to get the most out of life need to be able to deal with stress in an effective way so as not to be overwhelmed by it. But stress can also be experienced by under-achievers: the monotony of a quiet, boring life where nothing much happens and over which you seem to have no control can be as stressful, in a different way, as a high-powered life. This chapter is about taking control of stressful situations, or learning the skills to cope with them, in order to achieve balance in our lives. Working out solutions to stress allows you to control your reactions in any situation. Positive things will only happen if we take responsibility for our actions, and we are all capable of doing that. Our happiness is of our own making.

Positive thoughts lead to the kind of affirmation that can resolve stress. We can train ourselves in positve thinking: the brain is a muscle and we can train it to peak fitness just like any other muscle so that it is capable of handling difficult situations.

Abandon perfectionism

There is only one thing in nature that is perfect, and that is a snowflake. Arm yourself with this mantra: 'I'm not a snowflake'.

If you have the urge to be perfect go and lie down until the feeling goes away. The root of perfectionism lies in low self-esteem: 'I'm not good enough' and 'People won't like me unless…' The insecurity that arises from this self-perception is a driving force of ambition of competitiveness, and can lead to stress-related illnesses. It is a different matter to take pride in what you do, and to do it well, honing skills and stretching yourself to your full potential. This is admirable: but not in order to be better than anyone else, or in order to gain emotional control. Do it for its own sake, for the love of it, and the stress is removed. So examine your attitudes and see whether you want to adjust them.

The stress response

The body goes on full alert under stress and switches on a chain of biochemical changes which result in what is known as the 'fight or flight' reaction. This deeply rooted instinct dates back to times when humans would often have been faced with mortal danger from wild animals, and survival depended on lightning-quick responses. You either fight the sabre-toothed tiger or you run away as fast as you can – or maybe, you evolve a cunning strategy to trap it before it attacks you.

The endorphins released into the body under acute stress are endogenous morphines that kill pain and delay reactions, which is why, after a crisis, you collapse later in the day and your hands begin to shake at the very thought of what happened.

The stress hormones adrenalin and noradrenalin are released directly into the bloodstream producing a sudden surge of energy which enables you to fight the tiger, or to flee or to outwit it. Your heart rate increases (your heart thumps), and you may turn pale as blood vessels constrict. Blood pressure increases and so does the coagulation of the blood (you don't bleed so badly when it gets its claws into you). Breathing becomes faster and shallower, increasing oxygen intake which causes you to feel light-headed. You may experience increased sweating, nausea, as the digestive process is shut down and blood is diverted from the stomach, (you could develop ulcers if your encounters with tigers become too regular), and you will probably need to dash to the loo as the sphincter muscles of the bladder and bowel relax. The cortisol released acts on the liver to convert glycogen into blood sugar to produce the instant energy for flight, and mind and muscles go into overdrive as you and the tiger contemplate each other's destiny. Teeth grinding, foot tapping and nail biting are also common indicators of stress. Stress can obviously affect mood, too, fluctuating between anxiety, depression and anger. Irrational behaviour, disturbed sleep patterns, loss of short-term memory, emotional outbursts, lapses of concentration, over-reactivity and talking too loud or too fast are all manifestations of high stress levels.

STRESS CAN DAMAGE YOUR HEALTH

Chronic long-term stress can lead to enduring health problems from asthma to back pain to skin disorders. At a more serious level it can result in life-threatening illnesses like heart disease, cancer and strokes. Learning ability is impaired, and concentration diminished. Research experiments have even shown IQ levels to fall after exposure to long term stress.

Stress will probably hit us at our weak spot, the most delicate link in our system, whether that be the chest, head, low back or stomach. We will come to recognise that yet another headache or stiff back has an underlying cause in how we are living, which is calling out to be resolved. Never forget, stress is an infectious disease: we give it to the people who come close to us. So for the sake of others as well as ourselves, we need sensible strategies to deal with stress.

What stresses you?

The first step in coping with stress is to identify what stresses you most: the phone, the children, parents, money, noisy neighbours, travelling to work, being late, feeling guilty, divorce, trouble with in-laws, illness, retirement, sexual difficulties, trouble with the boss, a polluted environment, too much coffee, overeating, boredom, loneliness, unemployment, emotional overload, too much work, not enough time, not enough sleep, big exams, first job, a painful love affair, bereavement, moving house, Christmas… add your own triggers to this list.

Sit down for ten minutes and make a list of the things that you find most stressful about your life at the moment, starting with the worst. This will help you clarify your mind and find a strategy for change.

Christine, a succesful executive in her twenties, went through a patch of being impossibly stressed by her boss. But once she recognised why she was stressed by him, which buttons he was pressing, she understood that she could do something about it. She took action: she learned to pause, to breathe and observe her responses. She began to think more clearly. Her clarity of mind was improved by changing her diet: dropping caffeine, drinking less alcohol, and eating more fresh fruit and vegetables. This gave her more energy to deal with the situation.

When she realised that her reaction to her boss was partly just habit, she found she could teach herself a new habit, of looking at the problem in a positive way and overcoming negative responses. Focusing on this was at first difficult but ulimately immensely freeing. She found that saying a mantra to herself 'It's difficult – but I can do difficult things' worked wonders for her. She could! Her final freedom was the freedom to choose her attitude. We are what we think: attitude is all.

Once you create a space between yourself and your conditioned reaction, you can focus on how to deal with the stressor in a positive way. Armed with a positive attitude it is easier to take constructive action. You may not be able to eliminate the stressor altogether but you can change your reaction to it so it does not have deleterious effects on your own life and that of those closest to you.

Personality types

Psychologists describe three broad personality types. Most people possess qualities from all three types, with one in preponderance or in rare cases an equal balance. Recognising our own personality traits makes us more likely to be aware of our reactions to stressful situations, and more likely therefore to deal with them wisely. If you know that you have a habitual tendency towards anger, start to cultivate your easy-going side. If you are not assertive enough, practice the skills of standing up for yourself. Getting to know yourself better improves your quality of life.

TYPE A PERSON

Diana, a mother of two toddlers with a job in the film industry, is typical of a type 'A'.

She is notoriously stress-prone, and both her behaviour and lifestyle elicit constant arousal and stimulation.

Women like her tend to be ambitious, vigorous, competitive, impatient, aggressive and hard-working.

Diana sets high goals both for herself and for others, and thrives on the stress-induced hormone noradrenalin which makes her feel confident and elated, but she often suffers from anxiety.

She is addicted to stress and rarely pauses for long enough to wonder what effect tight deadlines and difficult board meetings are having on her.

TYPE B PERSON

Jennifer is more of a type 'B': a calm, easy-going mother of three and part-time social worker.

She is not overtly ambitious and less prone to symptoms of stress although she sometimes finds herself in the over-achieving mode, but in a less ambitious and hyperactive way than Diana.

She is certainly more stoical. People regard her as dependable and cheerful. She refuses to give in to illness, and cannot say no to demands made on her.

She is a perfectionist. Jennifer finds herself placing the needs of others before her own and can find it hard to express her deepest feelings.

She tends to deny the dangers of stress and is inaccurate in her assessment of her own limitations and vulnerability.

TYPE C PERSON

A type C person like Laura finds it difficult to express her emotions: she hides her anger, lacks assertiveness and always tries to comply with other people.

She avoids conflict, and although she is calm and rational, conventional and stoical, and usually 'nice' this masks a self-sacrificial tendency towards hopelessness. There is an air of resignation about her which is the product of 'learned helplessness'.

She is often quiet in company and feels uneasy in the spotlight, preferring others to take the initiative.

People who tend to behave like victims and martyrs come into this category.

The approval trap

Some women need to be cured of being too 'good', too 'nice'. We need to learn to say 'no'. If this is really difficult for you, then a short course in assertive communication could change your life and give you a composure and confidence that you had only dreamed of. Lack of self-confidence can severely damage your life.

Nobody can make you feel inferior without your consent
Eleanor Roosevelt

One of the major causes of stress is great expectations: our conditioning to be all things to all women (and men) is not good for our health and should come with a warning. The impulse to be perfect (what is that anyway?) is about as dangerous as standing at the edge of a cliff. Take a step back and save your life. Perform your multiple roles by all means, but learn to ignore the urge to do them better than anyone else.

GIVE UP GUILT

Many women fall into the approval trap too easily, wanting to please everyone, to be seen as 'perfect', caring too much about what other people think. It is immensely liberating to realise that you don't have to carry on doing this. It is *not* an act of selfishness to avoid the approval trap, it is a creative act of self-affirmation which can have a positive effect on those around you. It is a famous fallacy based on a denial that women – whether daughters, wives or working mothers – have no limitations or needs of any kind. Childhood conditioning came from playing happy families with dolls and the lesson was learned too well, so failure to perform in the prescribed multiple roles inevitably led to feelings of guilt. 'Guilty' is a largely female word (when did you last hear a man say he felt guilty apart from possibly when he was found out?) Guilt is a feeling and your feelings are dictated by your thoughts. Change them.

It is possible that when you do this, other people may throw *their* guilt at you and try to make you feel that you do not deserve to do what you are doing. You deserve. Be assertive. Go for that job opportunity even if it means that your partner may have to accommodate by helping out more at home. If they object, just remember that it is their guilt that they are chucking in your direction (at their woeful track-record on the home front or whatever) and continue to get your own way (nicely). Sometimes we care about the wrong things too much (the approval trap again). It is immensely freeing to say to oneself 'I don't care' (for example about what people might think) to become carefree about the things that do not actually matter when we look at the bigger picture.

Be in the here and now for a while, and enjoy it. Life usually brings us what we need. We spend too much time either regretting the past or anticipating the future. Our life is full of wonderful experiences and half the time we are not here in the present moment.

*Sitting quietly
doing
nothing spring
comes and
the grass grows
by itself*
Zen

Control – or cope?

Unless we begin with a right attitude we will never find a right solution
CHINESE PROVERB

To every problem there is a solution. If there isn't a solution it isn't a problem it's a fact of life. The essence of stress is loss of control in a difficult situation. Stress-related problems arise from believing that you can control a situation when you can't, or that you can't control it when you can. For example, you can control your thoughts, you could be more self-assertive, you can change your plans. But you can't control the weather, the traffic, other people's personalities, ageing or illness. *Taking control* of a stressful situation means that first you identify it, then decide what to do about it and finally take action. *Coping* with stress means realising that there is a limited amount that you can do about the situation, and deciding to make the best of it rather than letting it get on top of you.

The basic survival skill here is to nurture a healthy sense of 'self-altruism', to find a balance between our own needs and the needs of others. Time for you is of central importance (see Chapter 3).

Controlling stress

Controlling stress is about problem solving. The first step is to acknowledge that there is a problem. Then adopt a positive attitude. With a negative attitude you don't stand a chance.

It is clear that there is no one single solution to the problem of stress: what is stressful for you may be stimulating and exciting for the next person. What you need is to strike that difficult balance between too much challenge and too little.

This comes with a health warning: poor copers have lower natural killer cell activity than good copers. The physical effects of stress are greatly magnified when you feel out of control. Something has to give: either your health, or the stressor. The choice is yours.

Take a long cool look at what is going on in your life and find out what elements of the situation are controllable. Control implies empowerment and autonomy, the opposite of passivity and negativity. Although we are all of us in the driving seat of our own lives, we often assume problems, draw negative conclusions and feel the need to accommodate others. Becoming chronically over-stressed often means that you have stopped paying attention to who you really are. Believing that you can't control a situation when you can often stems from 'learned helplessness'. This is the quitting response, a giving-up reaction rooted in the belief that nothing you can do will make any difference. It conceals depression born of pessimism. It can come from a common family dynamic such as having a brilliant elder sister, and which still causes the child inside to say, 'There's nothing I can do'. This internal voice may be triggered by someone at work who regularly puts you down. 'It's no use...' but it may be actually. Practise saying 'I can'. Positive thoughts lead to affirmative action.

Are you your own worst enemy?

If you see yourself in any of the following, you may be setting yourself up to become a victim of stress but these are all patterns which you can do something about, (see *Coping with Stress* pages 78-83). Patterns of habitual thinking cause stress: do you…

CRITICISE YOURSELF?

Self-critical women who have a touch of the Type C (see page 71) in them tend to blame themselves when realistically it is not their problem or there is no blame to be apportioned.

FEAR AND DOUBT?

This is paralysing. My friend Isabel, every time she talks (or even thinks) about her mother-in-law, goes into 'learned helplessness' (see page 74), and becomes impotent and incompetent. She is an intelligent woman, but her essential terror of the woman, and her self-doubt in dealing with the situation, paralyses her.

NEED TO BE LIKED (TOO MUCH)?

How many people do you know (including perhaps yourself) who suffer from this? Some working women cannot differentiate between friendship and a professional relationship, and this merging of boundaries makes for problems. Men are better at this: they can argue with a colleague and have a drink with a friend. Same person.

NEED TO CONTROL?

Successful women share. They delegate. Anita Roddick delegates. If you succumb to the control freak that lurks in all of us you severely limit your potential: there simply is not enough time and energy to do everything well yourself.

GO INTO THE 'POOR ME' VICTIM MODE?

'No one's life has ever been as difficult as mine' is an indulgent and overdramatized thought process. The solution to this one is not to take antidepressants (they change nothing), but to identify and take responsibility for the core problem that produces this behaviour. It may not be that complicated.

FOCUS ON THE WORST?

I know someone (don't we all) who always sees the worst-case scenario. It's always 'terrible, awful, dreadful'. Things are never as bad as all that. She indulges in catastrophising, making mountains out of molehills, assuming the worst. Life's too short!

OVER-ANALYSE?

Analysis-paralysis as it is known in the trade is a great favourite among the type A high-fliers who are high on stress-hormones. Too much analysis can lead you astray. Save your energy. Be guided by your intuition: it's a safer bet.

OVER-GENERALIZE?

This is an evasion. 'People who…', 'Everyone always thinks…' etc. These unfocused statements can have an aura of authority but are usually ungrounded in fact and tend to be misleading. Bring the issue back from the general to the particular. Cite specific examples (and who is 'everyone', anyway?)

TAKE CRITICISM PERSONALLY?

Do you go on the defensive whenever you feel criticized or rejected? Learn to look at this constructively – often we become defensive when someone is hitting a sore spot. Listen to what someone is telling you: being positive rather than defensive is the key to unlocking this pattern.

Many people get their best ideas in the bath, on the golf course, or while travelling. So build space into your routine, whether it be listening to music, meditating or enjoying a walk in the park. Or sleep on a problem. Often if you give your brain a question to ponder as you drift off (and this works with relaxation too) it will quietly whirr away and come up with the solution. Space can be amazingly clarifying.

USE YOUR RIGHT BRAIN POWER

Sometimes approaching a problem with the left brain rationale (analysing, brain-storming, deducing, using logic) simply does not work. It is like banging your head against a brick wall. So instead try going for a long walk, or enjoy a swim. Or just watch a movie. It is amazing how by resting the left brain approach the right brain often pops up with a solution.

...OR TRY LEFT BRAIN SOLUTIONS

If the right brain approach is not appropriate in the circumstances, look to solving the core problem logically, (remembering that if there isn't a solution it isn't a problem: it's a fact of life to be reckoned with).

The first step in rational problem solving is to look behind the symptoms and analyse the underlying problem: ask who, when, what, why, where and how?

Secondly, work out what you want or need in relation to the problem – realistically, within your control to achieve. You may for example need more communication with and less negative feedback from a colleague or partner.

Thirdly, look at the options: you can negotiate, you can change your mind, you can accept the status quo, or you can leave and get out. Instead of moaning, take action – remembering that every option has a price tag!

Finally, make an action plan and work out a timescale within which to evaluate the new position and to adjust to it. Then reward yourself – and the other person if appropriate.

Balance right-brain time with left-brain time, rather than pushing yourself against the grain. My friend Jane – a successful potter and author – used to get highly stressed by the pressures of work until she understood that her working day could be transformed by allowing herself right-brain time. What she had thought of as 'indulgence' she now understands to be natural balance.

Coping with stress

Our perception is our reality. Changing one changes the other. If your perception of a problem is negative, you are set on a different behaviour loop from if you see it in a positive light. Changing the way you think gives you immense power over your own life. It is the single most important factor in dealing with stress: how we distress (with automatic thoughts) or de-stress (with problem-solving thoughts.)

Stop and think again. Replace habitual thinking with new, more appropriate problem-solving thoughts.

See the funny side. Resort to humour as the greatest stress reliever of all time, keeping perspective on **la comédie humaine** ***rather than seeing life as a tragedy.***

CHANGE YOUR ATTITUDE

You do have a choice. You can change unproductive thoughts, weed out the negatives and nurture the positives. Simple as it sounds, this may not be easy: habits have a powerful hold. But with awareness and persistence it is possible to change habits and over-write old memory traces in the brain.

Challenge your perception.
'I can't bear it'… 'I can bear it'.
'This always happens to me'… 'This happened to me before and I coped'.
'I'll lose my job'… 'It's a big change, there's a better job around the corner and I need a change.'

- **Avoid negative people – they undermine any attempts at positivity**
- **Recognise that other people do *not* have the right to ruin your day! Only your thoughts have the power to do that**
- **Ask yourself, 'What have I been saying to myself to make myself feel…?'**
- **Always remember the adage 'What doesn't break you, makes you'**
- **Reserve this positive and self-fortifying mantra for regular occasions: 'I haven't peaked yet'**
- **Avoid rigid vocabulary ('should', always', 'no-one/everyone' and – especially – 'can't')**

EMOTIONS

We create our own heaven and our own hell in how we self-talk, and transforming that self-talk is one of the most powerful tools in controlling emotion. Our perception is coloured by it: instead of angrily thinking 'Who does she think she is?', replacing it with 'Perhaps she's unaware of my previous conversation with our colleague' will dictate the outcome of the interaction.

Anger, fear, happiness and sadness are survival emotions which can become confusingly intertwined. Anger may mask fear, sadness sometimes contains elements of suppressed anger. Even happiness may have the seeds of revenge lurking.

By identifying emotions you become clearer about their source and more able to take appropriate and affirmative action. Remind yourself that it is not necessary to fight every battle. Let some things go. Or deal with anger by going for a brisk walk, or some vigorous housework… Controlling emotion does not mean suppressing it. You may bury your feelings for a time, even years, but they will emerge eventually so, when you are ready, clear your system of grievances. It is a very cathartic process.

BE MORE ASSERTIVE

Stand up for yourself. Stop being so nice. Being too nice can be stressful, and it usually means that you're not communicating your true feelings. It is often an evasion and can be exhausting. When you bring up a touchy subject with the boss, don't go into shrinking-violet mode or become over-emotional: stand your ground gently but firmly. Not being 'nice' doesn't mean you have to be nasty: there are nice ways of being not nice. But it means that you no longer have to put up with things without making a fuss, you no longer have to compromise yourself. Nor do you always have to agree with people, get sucked into situations you don't want, or avoid conflict.

- **Programme yourself to think positively about yourself in your relationship to others**
- **Give up asking permission**
- **Stop saying 'sorry' unnecessarily: what might seem polite to you may actually be a lack of self-confidence**
- **Cease carping on your own weaknesses and, rather, change your perception to notice and nourish your strengths**

Re-training in something completely new is an excellent way to build up the self-confidence that is the ground of assertiveness. Learn a language, chess, botany, Finnish grammar or whatever your choice. Continuing to learn through life, to keep the brain as fit as the body, not merely enhances self-esteem but greatly enriches life. Committing to new goals is incredibly revitalizing.

MAKE GOALS

Taking a wider perspective in times of stress can be helpful, encouraging you to invest in yourself and strengthen your self-esteem. If we ask ourselves some big questions it clarifies important goals and also helps determine our desired lifestyle and accomplishments. Apply these goals to family, friends, partners, and work alike. For example:

- **What is 'enough' as far as I am concerned?**
- **Where do I want to be in ten years' time?**
- **What would I actually do with time and money if I had lots of both?**
- **What do I want to accomplish in my lifetime?**
- **What do I want my long-term lifestyle to be?**
- **What do I want more or less of in my life?**
- **What are my weaknesses, what are my strengths and where can they take me?**
- **What is most important to me: work, family, friends, children...?**
- **What is the one thing I have never done but always wanted to do?**

Choose some long-term goals as well as some short-term ones. For times when your spirits flag a little, keep a collection of inspiring quotations or news stories which will spur you on to your goals when you need encouragement. It's called stress-inoculation by the medical profession: making use of positive coping statements, in this case other people's.

Learn to say NO, to buy time for yourself, don't bother to rise to the bait, and don't always worry about what people think. It's such a relief.

Favourite hobbies, listening to a great piece of music or reading a much-loved poet are other ways of resourcing yourself, as is indulging in activities that fill you with excitement and passion.

Surrounding yourself with people who make you feel good about yourself is a start: constant negative feedback undermines your attempts to deal positively with stress.

FRIENDS FRIENDS FRIENDS

Research experiments show that humans who have a social support network, suffer less under stress. If you don't have a supportive family, seek out friends to share your thoughts and feelings in a healthy two-way deal (but don't become a selfish moaner). Getting involved in an activity with others such as a tennis club or reading group will mean that feelings of isolation and 'why does this have to happen to me' diminish and relieve the symptoms of stress. The solidarity that friendship affords is of central importance: you can't put a price on friendship, so nurture your friends (see page 47).

THE PAUSE

Because reaction to stress is automatic, and often based on a past-programmed response, pausing creates a 'space of time' between the stressor and your reaction to it. It restores emotional control. Don't go into defensive mode: defensive is powerless. Showing confident body-language and keeping a steady eyeline with the other are both important factors in dealing with stressful situations. Say to yourself, 'I can handle this calmly' – and breathe.

- **Tell yourself, 'I'm all right, right now, in this situation'**
- **Breathe deeply, in though the nose and out through the mouth, relaxing the jaw**
- **Count to ten. In intense situations you can go to the Ladies' and do this for two minutes**
- **Never forget the Fifth Amendment. Silence can be a powerful weapon**

LET IT ALL OUT

If the above solutions don't work for you or are not appropriate, try letting it all hang out. Don't bottle up your stress, it will harm your brain and your body. We all need an outlet for stress. Do some strenuous physical activity or let loose with some verbal expression. Cry, scream, swear and even laugh hysterically, but chose carefully where and with whom you do this otherwise innocent victims will litter your life. Venting your frustration deactivates stress hormones and increases the production of antibodies, so you feel better immediately.

THE POWER OF NATURE

For times when things overwhelm you, you may need unconditional support, and personally I find this both in long walks in the countryside, and in animals. I turn to my wonderfully understanding dog, a superlative cat, and other peoples' horses. It is now well known that stroking a pet can bring down both blood pressure and cholesterol levels. Research at Melbourne University in Australia has shown that pets are not only good for your health but put years on your life too. Pet power is as great if not greater than the effect of exercise or diet, according to the Companion Animal Research Group at Cambridge University.

TAKE A DAY OFF

Cancel your appointments, and do what you want to do rather than what you think you ought to do. Take yourself off for a walk by the sea. You'll function twice as well the next day.

Aromatic oils for stressful times

A simple way to calm yourself is to put 2-3 drops of lavender or vetivert on a handkerchief and inhale deeply from time to time. Or if you need to ground yourself, a drop of frankincense or juniper on the palm of the hand, inhaled from time to time, works wonders.

Whether you put a few drops in the bath, burn some in a vaporiser or get an expert aromatherapy treatment, essential oils can alleviate stress in a most pleasurable way.

ANXIETY: basil and bergamot (uplifting), geranium (relaxing), lavender (soothing) and sandalwood (calming)

MILD SHOCK: chamomile (calming), rosemary (stimulating), melissa (anti-depressant), neroli and peppermint

DEPRESSION: bergamot, rosemary and sage (uplifting) camomile, jasmine, lavender, neroli, patchouli, sandalwood, ylang ylang

MENTAL FATIGUE: eucalyptus and peppermint (reviving), rosemary (for concentration)

DON'T SELF SABOTAGE

Take time out to be on your own and relax. Take better care of yourself, maybe by indulging in a good pampering (see page 190) Be kind to yourself, because if you learn to love yourself then other people will love you too. Insecure people who lack this skill are draining to be with. Visualise the outcome you most want to happen, in whatever issue is current: reconnect with your goals and sit quietly with them. Beware of blaming yourself for everything: we all make mistakes and have failures. Learn from them. Move forwards and don't look back.

Catch yourself when you start on your pattern of self-destruct and find an alternative. Instead of a shopping binge when you're broke, call a friend and meet for a coffee. Check negative thinking and listen to your intuition. Get in the habit of looking at both sides of an argument.

Learn to be spontaneous, rather than hiding behind routine. Routines can become prisons, whether at work or at home, and breaking out of them is liberating. Welcome change as opportunity and adventure.

RELAX

Be a Human Being for a change instead of a Human Doing! Recharge your batteries by meditation (see page 199), yoga or breathing exercises (see Chapter 5) and introduce your body to the relaxation response, the best antidote to the stress response. Relaxing is an essential life skill and is good for your health.

Instant stress busters

There are numerous quick-fixes that bring relief in acute stress, some mental, some emotional and some physical. For instant tension release, try dropping your head to your chest, breathing in as you lift the head to look forward, then breathing out as you drop the head back. Repeat three times. Or try any of the following...

- **Slow down and take your time. Talk, walk or drive at a slower pace**
- **Call a friend for a long chat**
- **Escape mentally – read a novel, watch a movie, be a sports spectator**
- **Keep a notebook on you and make lists: being disorganised is stressful**
- **Look at some wonderful paintings (or paint something yourself)**
- **Change into comfortable clothes**
- **Help someone. Be really nice to someone**
- **Take a power-snooze (see page 97)**
- **Get a massage or a pedicure. Or just stroke the back of your hand gently – DIY Zone Therapy**
- **Take time out: walk around the block, hum your favourite song, phone your mum. Then get back to your stressful activity**
- **Write a rage letter and don't send it**
- **Find a safe place to cry. Crying restores the chemical balance of the body**
- **Drop perfectionism: it stresses you out**
- **Stroke the dog or the cat**
- **Shut the door on the world at least once a day and see to your own needs: do some yoga or meditation**
- **Lie down with a hot wet flannel over your face**
- **Go away for a long weekend**
- **Smile. It relaxes the major facial muscles and releases serotonin from the brain and makes you feel better**
- **Lie in a hot tub and add soothing essential oils (see page 174) to the water. Dim the lights, light a candle, and breathe. Dab lavender oil on your temples**
- **Stop thinking 'must' 'should' and 'ought' for at least an hour**
- **Sweat out your stress. Take some vigorous exercise, dance till you drop**
- **Write a list of all the essential things you have to do – then stick it on the fridge and leave it until tomorrow**
- **Your mobile phone is a power-tool. Switch it off to prevent someone using that power over you**
- **Sometimes doing nothing is the key to stress**
- **Go shopping: indulge in the most popular alternative medicine of all, retail therapy**
- **Express yourself: don't maintain the stiff upper lip. And don't lose your sense of humour**
- **Change your routine – have a beautiful bath (see pages 169-170) mid afternoon**
- **Do some gardening**
- **Cancel all your appointments and take a day off**
- **Collect inspirational quotations and stories and refer to them to lift your spirits**

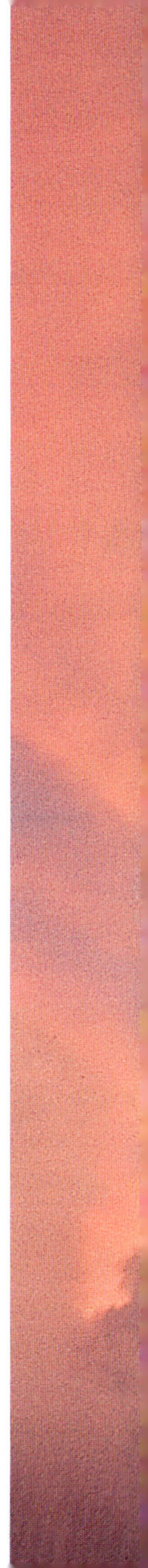

TIPS FOR STRESS-FREE ENTERTAINING

Planning: the key is organisation. Think ahead.

Cook in advance where possible.

Keep the menu simple. People come for the company as much as for the food.

Be ready well before your guests arrive – table laid, food prepared, yourself changed and ready – and above all calm. Even the simplest of flower arrangements, or even just foliage, make special touches.

Don't be afraid to delegate. Most people love to help!

A little of what you fancy

The Associates for Research Into the Science of Enjoyment (ARISE), based at Reading University, study the nature and effects of pleasure and have investigated its value as an antidote to the stress brought on by unnecessary guilt. Put at its simplest, pleasurable activities release the natural chemical serotonin into the body leading to feelings of well-being and enhanced good mood. Family and children rate high on the pleasure scale, and reading, entertaining friends, drinking tea, coffee or alcohol, visiting people and going out for a meal all play an important part. Soaking in a hot bath, taking exercise, doing yoga and meditation are popular too.

'There is clear evidence' says Professor David Warburton, the co-ordinator of ARISE, 'that a cup of coffee, a glass of wine and a few pieces of chocolate make people calmer, more relaxed and generally happier. Medical evidence shows that happier people live longer, so moderate indulgence can only be beneficial.' We do well to bring pleasure into the balance of our lives – naturally in moderation: over-indulgence can harm yourself and others. We all know what is good for us, and what makes us feel better: so why go to the trouble of feeling guilty about it? (We also know what makes us feel worse: that entire packet of chocolate biscuits is a disaster.)

Pleasure has an important role in the healthy regulation of behaviour, both physically and mentally. Apparently 43 per cent of us would enjoy our everyday pleasures more if we did not feel so guilty. But pleasure is a great investment: it has its mirror image in performance, and we are more likely to give pleasure to those around us when we allow it, in balance, into our lives.

Anhedonia – the absence of a capacity to experience pleasure – is a dangerous condition and can seriously damage your health. So the wise old adage of 'a little bit of what you fancy does you good' is sound advice to restore balance to a busy life.

TRAVEL TIPS

When making an unfamiliar journey, work out the route first and write out the road numbers in sequence on a sticky label. Putting it on to the steering wheel as you drive could save a life: reading a map solo while driving is not a good idea.

Listen to audio-books instead of relentless radio, and transform your driving time with something really thrilling or interesting.

Stretch, relax, exercise

Natural exercise

Both body and mind benefit from exercise. 'Every time I feel like taking exercise I go and lie down until the feeling passes,' wrote Oscar Wilde. This epigram is, however, imbued more with wit than wisdom. Exercise is vital. There is a recognized, and measurable, link between fitness, stress levels, and both intellectual and emotional well-being. Its mood-enhancing effect, and immune-protection function mean that we are healthier, happier and more alert individuals with some form of regular physical activity.

Energy is the power that drives every human being. It is not lost by exertion but maintained by it.
GERMAINE GREER

THE BENEFITS OF EXERCISE

Exercise, even gentle forms, makes muscles stronger and more toned, and your posture also improves so you have a better shape and appearance. Exercise increases bloodflow to the brain supplying it with essential oxygen and glucose which improves mental agility and learning capacity. A well-exercised body has 500ml more blood than a poorly exercised one and since the brain uses 25 per cent of all the blood in the body, almost any exercise helps improve its function. It has even been shown to improve memory. Exercise stabilizes blood sugar, reduces blood pressure and results in a lower resting pulse rate, giving you a 20 per cent lower risk of heart disease. It burns up body fat, and strengthens heart and lungs.

Importantly for women, exercise helps maintain bone density thus reducing the risk of osteoporosis, and one quarter of stroke incidence can be avoided by taking regular exercise. It is also an effective means of weight control.

On a psychological level, exercise has been shown to be more effective than traditional therapies, including counselling, for many conditions. The endorphins released by physical activity substantially decrease depression and anxiety, and improve sleep patterns. Increasing numbers of doctors are prescribing exercise rather than drugs as an antidote to depression, so go for a brisk walk and let your natural brain chemicals do the job for you.

With exercise you feel better, look better and have a better body image. It improves self-esteem and gives you more confidence, and you feel a marked increase in your energy level. People who take regular exercise experience less stress than those who don't, and feel, according to findings reported by the British Psychological Society, happier in their work. You are better able to cope with stress because your reactivity to stressors decreases.

Exercise boosts energy and stamina, and the experts agree that half an hour per day of moderate activity is all you need for the effect to kick in – brisk walking, gentle jogging, rowing, swimming, riding, cycling, skating, martial arts or tennis. It needs to be regular – intermittent exercise does not have the same effect.

Another way of looking at it is to think of exercise as being ecologically friendly: if you walk, jog or cycle to work you are reducing the number of times you use energy-consuming vehicles, and thus make less impact on the environment. Exercise boosts your metabolism and generates heat, so you become less dependent on external sources such as central heating to keep you warm. Its generally health-giving effects will mean fewer visits to the doctor and no need to resort to minor drugs or props of any kind to make you feel better.

DO IT NATURALLY

A professional woman working for a publishing company described how, bleary in the early morning, she would drag herself along to a particularly nasty-looking building where music was throbbing, the TV was on and sweaty bodies competed for muscle tone. Once attached to heart monitor and speed metre she was made to do painful and uncomfortable movements that made her body feel terrible. She sweated so heavily that she had to change all her clothes and wash her hair, against the clock, and finally left feeling ghastly in both body and mind. And she'd paid through the nose for the privilege.

What this woman really needed was a form of exercise which suited her body, her biorhythms (see page 40) and her lifestyle. For example, a solitary walk where she could think her thoughts and go at her chosen pace.

A brisk walk early in the morning before work gets the day off to a positive start and many health experts recommend it as a panacea for practically everything. You have two doctors: your left leg and your right leg. I regularly walk up the hill before breakfast, in most weathers, really moving my body and feeling the fresh air push through my system. It clears the head, refreshes and wakens the body, raises energy, calms the mind, ups the metabolism, gets rid of sluggishness, lifts the spirits and strengthens the will. It is a lovely time to exercise, in the freshness of a new day before the world wakes up: after a night's sleep the body needs the movement, the soul needs the space, and the brain needs oxygen, which it gets through increased breathing and heart rate. You feel energised and fresh (oxygen works). And it's free.

TAKE IT EASY

Extreme physical exertion can actually do more harm than good and may provide little or no enjoyment. But there are gentle ways of strengthening and balancing the body which can also be hard work. Tai chi, chi gong, yoga (see pages 102-115), pilates, dancing and breathing exercises (not to be underestimated) are some. Even some gentle stretching first thing in the morning as you are waiting for the shower to run can improve flexibility and strength (see pages 158-159). Climbing stairs regularly at a good pace counts too – so ignore the lift. Or walk that short bus ride. Energetic spring-cleaning does the trick too. (If you think that you are actually looking after your health as well as your home, you may be slightly more inspired to get on with the hoovering!)

These forms of exercise can be done in the course of everyday life, and don't take up a lot of time. You simply have to programme them into your day just as you do for brushing your teeth or doing your hair.

ENJOY YOUR EXERCISE

Natural exercise substitutes positive for negative addictions: the latter – drugs, nicotine, alcohol and even TV – have a cost on both health and social life. Exercise is a positive force in your life so whichever form you choose, you are more likely to keep it up if it is a refuge from the stresses of life. Be gentle on yourself and have a playful attitude to your exercise time. Half an hour per day of moderate activity is all you need for the effect to kick in. The important thing is to enjoy your chosen form of exercise, to find what suits you so that it becomes a pleasure and not a torment. Listen to your body. So however busy you are, you do well to make time for exercise: beginning may be hard, but the rest is easy.

Using your body well

Most of us abuse our bodies much of the time simply by the carelessness with which we use them in everyday life. We sit badly, we lie awkwardly in bed, we neglect our posture, we walk around with tense necks and shoulders, we stagger to work with a heavy brief-case in one hand, and we crucify our feet in ill-fitting shoes. But we ignore the body at our peril. Becoming aware of small details as you carry out everyday tasks can make a big difference to your overall health and energy, and keep you in balance to cope with the demands of a busy life. This awareness is not time-consuming, it is simply a matter of adjustment.

THE ALEXANDER TECHNIQUE

'Use promotes function' is the theory evolved by F. T. Alexander as he formulated his now-famous technique. The Alexander Technique is a subtle re-training of the body which brings awareness to the head-neck-back relationship. It teaches you to lengthen, to go up not down, to free the neck, and to expand and widen the back (see *Useful Addresses* page 204). This re-education frees the body to stand well, to feel light, to find its natural alignment. If you use your body well you improve its functioning. To eliminate old habits you first have to become aware of what you are doing wrong. The balanced use of the body also achieves mental and emotional balance as the body-mind tensions dissolve.

Basic posture

Posture is 'good' when it is aligned yet relaxed. By adjusting into a more upright stance you will feel more energetic. Distortions in posture will affect your breathing because of compression of the lungs, as well as constricting the heart and impeding its full function. Abdominal muscles will sag causing aches and pains. Excessive weight carried around the abdomen causes a forward pelvic tilt and will result in tension and pain in the lower back, so it is important to reduce weight there and also to exercise and strengthen abdominal muscles.

Think of a spruce tree: ground level is waist high, the legs are the roots, the spine the slender trunk growing upwards and from which everything else can relax down. The essence of the experience is that your feet are being pulled down into the ground without effort, while the head grows tall towards the sky. Through connecting with gravity in this way you experience the elongation of the spine.

TALL, ALIGNED, RELAXED

- **In a good posture an imaginary line connects your ear, shoulder, hip, knee and ankle, and your shoulders and hips are level**
- **To stand in a relaxed state of alignment, take the feet hip-width apart, keeping them straight**
- **Open the knees, and imagine the back of your pelvis moving down away from the waist, with the spine lengthening upwards away from the pelvis**
- **If you lock the knees the pelvis tilts forward and hollows the back: feel that the curve in the back of the waist is as flat as possible**
- **Lift the sternum but relax the shoulders**
- **Your centre of gravity is in the lower abdomen. Imagine you are an egg timer: from the hip bones down, gravity pulls your legs and feet into the ground. From the hip bones up, anti-gravity operates, so that the spine feels light and free, the shoulders relaxed**
- **Feel the ground under your feet and become aware of your feet expanding and growing roots**
- **Now imagine that you are being pulled up to the ceiling by an invisible thread attached to the crown of the head**

Sitting in a chair

Choice of chairs affects your sitting habits: the seat must not be too deep: you need to be able to sit comfortably with the back well supported and the feet resting squarely on the floor. The chair should align the knees just lower than the hips (if the knees are higher the back slumps, and if too low, the lumbar arches). Instead of slumping, lengthen the spine away from the hips, pull your chin in slightly, free the neck and imagine the head being pulled up by a single hair, leaving shoulders open and relaxed. Inhale into the back, expanding your back ribs. As a general rule, don't remain sitting in the same position for very long at one time: the intra-discal pressure while sitting is greater than when standing, the spine more jammed up because the base is immobilised on to a seat. Use posture wedges for the back of straight seats to allow for and to support the natural curve of the spine.

GETTING IN AND OUT OF CHAIRS

Always have one foot in front of the other when getting out of a chair.

Slide your hips to the edge, then with spine vertical and chin dropped slightly, free the neck, then lengthen and widen the back as you use your thigh muscles and arms to bring yourself to standing.

SITTING AT WORK

It is astonishing how little thought or awareness goes into designing comfortable positions for sitting in front of computers or working at tables. Often we distort the body by pulling the head forward, tightening the shoulders and dropping the feet back under the chair. There is an invisible geometry of sitting at the computer: your eyeline should be horizontal to the monitor. The upper arm should fall vertically, the lower arm should be horizontal. Your spine should be upright, your lower legs vertical and the feet flat on the floor.

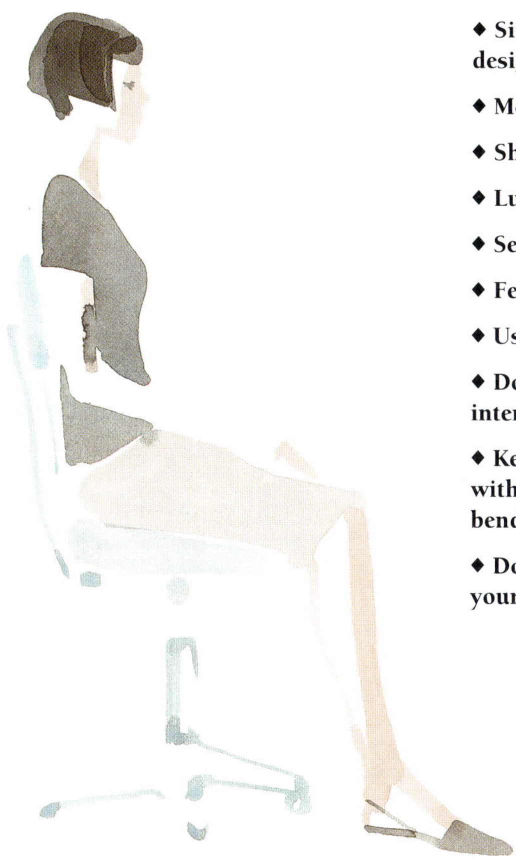

CHOOSING A CHAIR FOR WORK

Your chair must allow you to sit well back in it with an upright back, but be comfortable enough for you to relax, with some support for the lumbar spine.

The edge of the seat must not cut into the back of the thigh, so it is best if it slopes down slightly to tilt the pelvis forward.

The height should be set at where you can put the feet comfortably flat on the floor.

AT THE COMPUTER

- **Sit well (see illustration) in a well-designed chair for the purpose**
- **Monitor at eye-level**
- **Shoulders relaxed, arms at right-angles**
- **Lumbar support in chair**
- **Seat sloping gently**
- **Feet flat on the floor**
- **Use a sloping desk or keyboard**
- **Do simple exercises at regular intervals (see pages 94-95)**
- **Keep most frequently used objects within easy reach to avoid awkward bending**
- **Don't cradle the telephone between your neck and shoulder**

A 'balans' chair helps to encourage correct posture and keeps the spine naturally aligned. It is however hard on the knees so you need to spend only short periods using it. My ideal solution is to have two working chairs: one well-designed chair with adjustments, for writing at my table, and a balans chair for working on the computer. I move in and out of them regularly and the change in position is always a relief.

Spontaneous stretches

Like any machine, the body needs care and maintenance, and one aspect of this care is to stretch and relax in between concentrated bouts of work. Animals do this as a matter of course, and it is a natural need that we neglect at our peril. Repetitive Strain Injury (RSI) is an example of what happens when we mercilessly repeat restricted movements with no rest and no stretching in between. This excruciating inflammation of the tendons is caused by locked muscles and tendons chafing against each other.

Stand with feet slightly apart. Interlock fingers behind your back, then bend forward bringing the arms up as far as you can behind the shoulders. Stretch the legs.

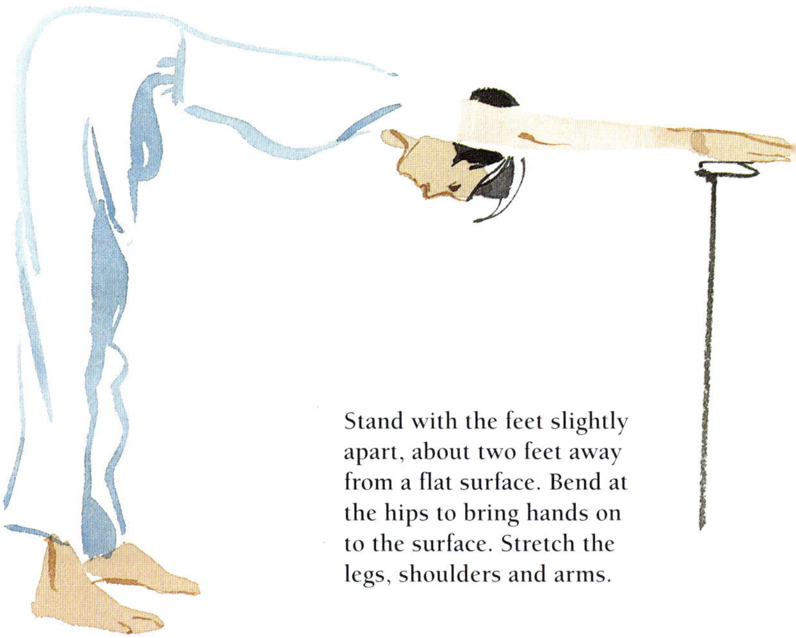

Stand with the feet slightly apart, about two feet away from a flat surface. Bend at the hips to bring hands on to the surface. Stretch the legs, shoulders and arms.

Sitting on a chair with feet apart, interlock fingers, turn hands outwards, and bring your arms straight up over your head. Look up and stretch the hands to the ceiling.

This stretch is for Repetitive Strain Injury in the wrist. Stand with feet slightly apart. Bring arms out to shoulder level and point the fingers up to the ceiling. Stretch strongly into the wrists.

Sit on the edge of your chair with legs wide apart. Drop the trunk towards the thighs and let the head hang loosely. Drop your arms loosely beside the legs.

Day-to-day living

Most of the time we go around as if the body isn't there. We are oblivious to how we are using or mis-using it. And we pay a price: stiff necks and sore backs are complaints that most of us are familiar with. Developing an awareness of the relationship between head, neck and back is crucial for good body use, for co-ordination and balance. The famous Alexander Technique maxim of 'free the neck so that the back can lengthen and widen and the head go forward and up' applies to most day-to-day situations.

STANDING FOR LONG PERIODS

This can kill your back if you don't stand well. Stand with the legs at hip width apart to give you maximum support and stability, releasing your knees and adjusting your alignments to true vertical. Pull the abdominal muscles back to flatten the lumbar curve. Shift the weight gently from one foot to the other. Use gravity (see *Basic Posture* page 91).

◆ If you are cooking or standing at the sink for a long time, or ironing, place one foot up on a box about 23 cm (8 in) high and solid enough to take your weight. This relieves the back and avoids tension. Change to the other foot as needed

HOUSEWORK

Housework generally involves putting the body into awkward positions and making restricted movements which are heavy on the back.

General tips include never bending over from the waist to load the dishwasher or washing machine, to make the bed etc. Kneel or squat instead. Take your time, and keep your abdominal muscles braced. Make sure the ironing board is at the right height i.e. so that elbows are at right-angles to the board. Sit on a high stool rather than stand.

The same applies to work-surfaces in the kitchen: when standing for long periods cooking or ironing, put one foot up on to a block to take the strain off the lower back

◆ Use the Spontaneous Stretches (see pages 94-95) often

LIFTING AND CARRYING

Simple: never lift anything, whether heavy or light, with your legs straight. Always bend the knees when you lift something, making the big muscles of the leg do the work rather than imposing the strain on the delicate configuration of the lower back. Keep the weight of the object close to your body, and once upright keep the back as straight as possible.

Carry things evenly in both hands, don't for example always carry a heavy briefcase in your left hand only because it puts such a strain on that side of the body. Change from side to side to even up the work of the muscles and the strain on the intervertebral discs. Better still, use a backpack.

◆ If you have low back pain, don't lift anything. Get other people to do it for you, even the shopping

LYING IN BED AND SLEEPING

Make sure that your bed is neither too hard nor too soft. It needs to be firm but with a little 'give' for the back to be able to relax. If possible, lie on one side or the other, slightly curled up, to release the lumbar spine. If you suffer from low back pain, put a cushion between your knees: this takes the strain off the lower back. Sleeping on your front can cause tension there but if you do like to sleep this way, put a pillow under your hips to minimize the pressure. If you sleep on your back, putting a pillow under the knees helps keep the lower back flat.

Have a pillow flexible enough to mould into the curve in your neck – down or feather-and-down work well – and feel that the muscles of the neck are supported in a neutral position. These small details can give you a deeper and more refreshing sleep, a must for women who are always on the go.

When getting out of bed, never pull yourself up into a sitting position from lying, because you are likely to overstrain your lower back. Instead, turn onto one side with the knees bent up. Then bring yourself to the upright position supporting yourself with your hand and arm. Then stand, following the principles of getting up out of a chair (see page 92).

♦ If you want to take a power-snooze during the day, instead of crashing out in a chair or sofa in a heap, try position 5 on page 105 or position 5 on page 109: both will add to the refreshment of the sleep and leave you stretched and aligned instead of crumpled afterwards!

IN THE CAR

Relax! Drop your shoulders, don't clutch at the wheel with your hands, release the fingers lightly. Feel the arms relax. Relax the jaw – don't clench the teeth. Relax the face. Breathe. Do the mindful breathing (see page 200) if you are in a hurry or stuck in traffic.

Have a lumbar support for the driver's seat – a small cylindrical pillow that can be strapped to the back of most seats makes a huge difference to how you feel afterwards, particularly if you do a lot of driving. You can also use it for watching TV, or at work, or for reading.

♦ Make sure the driver's seat is tilting backwards slightly – an upright seat will put a lot of pressure on your lumbar discs

GARDENING

Get help to do the heavy work: protect your back. Don't bend from the waist: kneel to weed. Take a waterproof cushion around the garden with you.

♦ Squat to reach down: don't bend. Stretch out afterwards (see pages 94-95)

WALKING

Make sure your posture is reasonable (see page 91). Keep your feet straight rather than turning them out, to avoid distortion of the leg and hip muscles. Relax the upper body and let your arms swing loosely from the shoulders in time with your pace. Let go of your shoulders and let the hips do the moving. Feel your feet touching the ground for a change!

♦ Keep your hands relaxed and maintain an even pace with your head balanced. Think relaxed, light and loose

Stretches for painful backs

Between 75 per cent and 80 per cent of us experience low back pain at some time in our lives. Women who have too much to do are among the most prone to this debilitating condition since they are often under stress, and may not make enough time to look after their backs. As this chapter will show, you can do so for no cost and very little time involved. Low back pain can be of sickening intensity, draining your energy. Every year in the UK alone back problems cause over a hundred million days off work and take up many millions of medical consultations. Yet 50 per cent of back pain remains undiagnosed and is largely treated with painkillers, or, at worst, surgery. Analgesics and muscle-relaxants can relieve symptoms but are not the best long-term answer because of their effect on lifestyle, and insidious side-effects.

Your back needs maintenance, whether or not you suffer or have suffered from back pain. The body is a machine, and machines need, for proper functioning, rest, exercise and maintenance. We look after our cars, we spend time and money on making sure that they are properly serviced so that they run well and give us optimum performance. Most of us don't consider giving that treatment to our own bodies... so why not look after your back as well as you look after your car? For free.

The causes of low back pain are well-known. Poor posture, being overweight, inactivity, lack of abdominal strength, arthritis, osteoporosis, osteomyelitis and other spinal conditions are common culprits. Undoubtedly too, psychological stress is a component, borne out over and over again by backs 'going' in a crisis or under the strain of long-term stress. Certainly lifting heavy objects, driving for long periods, sitting or standing for a long time, carrying children, making sudden movements, getting out of bed the wrong way (see page 97), heavy housework, even sneezing can trigger back pain. And what a gardener needs is a cast-iron back with a hinge in it.

Everyone's back is different and so is the course of their back pain, therefore different remedies apply to everyone. Nonetheless, in my experience of working over the years with people who suffer from bad backs, the following stretches have helped most of them. They show you how to help yourself in bouts of back pain, they relieve the tightness of spasm, and strengthen the muscles that support the back. The relief from pain is achieved by simple movements, with breathing, which also alleviate the stiffness and discomfort triggered in other parts of the back. They were worked out in collaboration with an eminent sports physiotherapist and have been checked over by a top neurologist.

You can incorporate the stretches quite easily into everyday life: just a few minutes a day will maintain the improvement, keeping the spine supple and the back muscles strong. 'A little and often' is a good rule and will lead you to an awareness of how to look after your back in everyday life.

There will never be a single cure for back pain – whoever dreams that one up will make themselves a fortune by solving an age-old problem – but you will help yourself by proper methods of stretching, standing, sitting and sleeping (see pages 92-97). Maintenance is the key.

GET YOURSELF COMFORTABLE

Choose a quiet, clean, warm place where you will not be interrupted by the telephone or the family. Programme stretching into your daily routine. If you don't, it won't get done. The best times are first thing in the morning, and last thing at night in order to go to sleep relaxed. Then try to find ten minutes in the middle of the day to loosen and relax.

Stretching must be done using the breathing. Never hold your breath while stretching – your body tenses up in response and that causes more tension not less. Never stretch against or into pain. This will damage the tissues and/or increase inflammation (see *The Stretch Reflex on* page 103).

FOR SEVERE PAIN

Lie down on a thick, evenly-folded blanket, pillows or duvet. In acute cases you can do these stretches on your bed, but the sooner you can work on a firm surface the better.

Put a low pillow underneath the head and mould it into the curve at the back of the neck.

Check that your body is straight, with the feet to the floor, hip-width apart, the knees up. Don't lie flat with the legs stretched out – this puts pressure on the lower spine and can make your symptoms worse.

◆ **Hold each stretch for three deep breaths on each side, and remember to do them slowly and gently**

The stretches should feel good. Never over-do it. This isn't 'exercise', it's stretching and relaxing. Nor is it a contest: there are no prizes. So stretch without strain or stress – keep it relaxed.

1. Relax the shoulders and let the head drop into the pillow. Allow the trunk to sink into the floor.

Soften the eyes and allow them to rest. Release the jaw, and relax the whole face.

Follow the breath, placing the hands on the belly and observing the rise and fall of the abdomen. Breathe in softly, breathe out deeply, releasing on the exhalation as if on a sigh or a yawn, breathing through the pain.

2. Carefully bring the right knee towards you. Hold the leg around the back of the thigh and as you exhale draw the right knee towards the right side of the chest. Repeat on several exhalations. Replace the foot gently. Repeat for several exhalations on the other side.

Keep all the movements slow, gentle and careful so as not to exacerbate your pain.

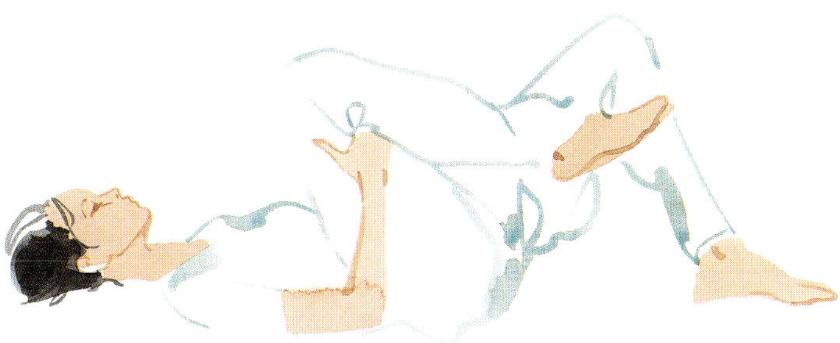

3. One leg at a time, gently bring both knees towards the chest. Hold around the backs of the thighs. Exhaling, feel the lower back lengthening at the end of each exhalation, relaxing the lower back muscles and loosening and releasing the tension there. The breath is like the oil of the machine, loosening it and helping it to work smoothly and freely. Take the knees around in little circles to massage the lower back into the floor.

Low back pain causes a lot of tension in the shoulders, since they react by holding on and tightening to protect the lower back. These stretches do wonders to release that tension.

4. Now bring the feet and knees together, still with the knees bent and feet to the floor. Stretch the right arm out at shoulder level, and turn the head to look at it. Now take the knees towards the left elbow all the way down to the floor. Breathe as before, exhaling to soften and release. After thirty seconds come carefully back to the centre and repeat to the other side. As your back improves you can do this with the legs crossed, or knees bent towards the chest.

5. Lying on your back put the left foot to the floor with the knee bent, and cross the right ankle over the knee. With both hands, draw the left knee towards you (the right hand goes through the triangle-shape created by the right leg). Keep the neck and shoulders relaxed, and breathe into the lower back and hips. It is a big stretch. Repeat on the other side.

6. Lie on your back with the right leg stretched out and the left foot on the floor by the right knee. Take your left arm out at shoulder level and bring the left knee over torwards the floor on the right side. Hold it down gently with your right hand. Turn to look at your left hand and breathe into the stretch. Repeat on the other side.

7. Then turn over onto your side, still with the knees bent so that you are in the foetal position. Roll over into a kneeling position and go into the Child Pose (see illustration below).

CHILD POSE

Kneel. Sit back on your heels and stretch the trunk forward over the thighs to bring the forehead to the floor. Take the arms back beside the body with the palms up so that the hands rest beside the feet.

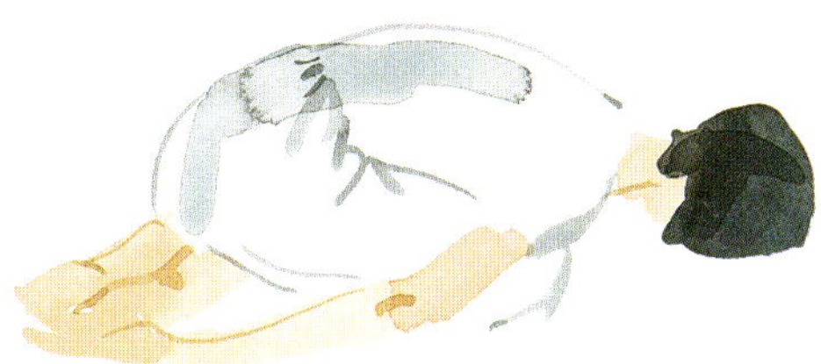

Don't do this posture if you have knee problems.

You can place a pillow under the forehead and let the whole face relax as you close the eyes and breathe in this posture.

To make the pose more comfortable:
if your buttocks don't touch your heels put some cushions on your heels until you can rest the bottom comfortably. Relax onto the cushions.
you may need to take the knees slightly apart. Keep the feet together, open the knees and you will find that you can drop forward more easily so that the forehead rests on the pillow. Make it higher if you are still not comfortable.

Yoga

Yoga originated in northern India some five thousand years ago as a path for spiritual development. The word yoga means to join, a union or integration of body and mind with the spiritual ground of existence. It also means to yoke, implying a discipline of mental and physical purification which makes the body a fit temple for the soul. Equilibrium is the fruit of this practice.

Yoga postures and breathing, the elements of yoga best known to the west, work with the three forces of existence or *gunas* (see page 136). *Sattva* – illumination, calm and intelligence; *Rajas* – movement, activity and motivation; *Tamas* – solidity of matter, inertia and darkness. These correspond to the breath, the spine and the ground, essential elements in a yoga practice. The balance of the intricate body-mind connection manifested in yoga unites the intelligence of the head with the wisdom of the heart, where you experience a state of calm silence and unconditional joy.

THE EIGHT LIMBS OF YOGA

Yoga is an ethical philosophy whose tenets were expounded by Patanjali in his Yoga Sutras. Not much is known about this great sage, even his dates, estimated at anywhere between 200B.C. and 200A.D. He described the 'eight limbs' of yoga as *Yama* (restraints: non-violence, non-greed, truthfulness, non-covetousness, and chastity), and *Niyama* (observances: cleanliness, contentment, self-discipline, self-study, and attention to the divine). These are the roots of the tree and the foundation of the practice of yoga. Next come *Asanas*, the numerous physical postures designed both to purify and balance the body, and to train and discipline the mind; then *Pranayama*, or control and regulation of the breath, which brings it to oneness with the mind. Further up the tree comes *Pratyahara*, the control of the senses which leads to emancipation from desire, then *Dharana*, a single-pointedness which leads to mental equilibrium and non-attachment. Further up still comes *Dhyana* or meditation, a state of blissful communion with the divine; and finally *Samadhi* where body and senses are at complete rest and the practitioner goes beyond consciousness, fully alert, and experiences 'the peace that passes all understanding'.

WHY DO YOGA?

Put simply, you always feel better after doing yoga. The stretches convert negative energy – sluggishness, fatigue, inertia – into positive energy – vitality, freshness and lightness – overcoming any inherent dullness in the body. Yoga affects mind, mood, body, will and spirit in a positive way, due to, among other things, the hormonal activity triggered from the brain. Scientific research in Europe and the USA is just now beginning to verify the holistic benefits of yoga. Yoga works on the meridians of the body, undoing the blockages in them, making the energy flow freely and in balance, and the effect of a single practice can last well over twenty four hours. This is why you invariably have more energy and vitality after even a hard-working yoga practice. You don't lose energy, you create it. Moreover, the quietening effect of breathing practices relaxes the nervous system as well as increasing oxygen levels and blood supply to the internal organs. This brings immediate calm, tranquillity and mental clarity, and in the long term inner peace and equilibrium in both good and difficult circumstances.

Yoga de-toxes the body by speeding up the removal of waste and unwanted toxins. All the internal processes function smoothly in response to the work: twisting, turning upside down, bending forward, sideways and backward have the effect of a self-massage at all levels of the system. For example, inverted postures like the headstand and the shoulderstand literally flush out the major organs of the of the body with the help of gravity. Doing twists feels like squeezing out a dirty dishcloth. A long shoulderstand at the outset of a cold can make it disappear.

Yoga de-stresses you both physically and mentally as the body responds to the relaxation response. Once you incorporate a regular stretching routine into your life you will find that you have more stamina and are less prone to illness. The fact that you can give yourself this gift every day – with its resulting tranquillity and mental clarity – is one of the underestimated wonders of life.

THE STRETCH REFLEX

When you overstretch or stretch too quickly, without breathing, nerve reflexes respond by sending a message to the muscles involved, telling them to contract instantaneously. Thus you actually contract the muscles you are trying to lengthen, thereby damaging them by tearing micro-fibres (or worse). It's the same involuntary muscle contraction that occurs when you touch something hot: you instantaneously retract as a result of messages received by the proprioceptive receptors in the muscle.

Be soft and relaxed, with your attention on the muscles being stretched. Don't bounce in the stretches, and don't stretch to the point of pain. Exhale into the stretch where you feel it the most: the out-breath is a release (like a sigh or a yawn) and helps the muscles to let go of tension. Stretching should feel good.

Keep your eyes soft, using the 'peripheral vision' that enhances right-brain function so that you work in 'feeling' rather than 'thinking' mode.

Doing yoga keeps the body in better health. There is no old age. Indeed, you can start yoga at any age: done in the right way, using the breath and gravity, you will never damage the body.
VANDA SCARAVELLI

TADASANA

Tadasana means mountain, and is the basic standing posture (see page 91) from which to go into standing *asanas*. You will find that it is the essence of all the other postures: gravity, lightness, breath. Tadasana aligns the spine so that you have maximum length between the sacrum and the top of the neck (occiput), and balances the crown of the head exactly over the sacrum. This frees the spinal energy from any blockages.

A daily yoga practice

This short programme of yoga *asanas* can serve as a prompt for a regular practice. Ideally, find a good teacher and go to a weekly class, then use this daily practice as a guide. Programme your practice into your day and stick to it so that it becomes as much of a routine as brushing your teeth. 'Allow your practice to be beautiful,' said the great yoga teacher Vanda Scaravelli. Remember that your body and your stretches are individual to you – there is no standard to which to aspire, no 'perfect state', just the freedom to be yourself and feel good about it. Give yourself a treat.

Attach no other importance to the posture other than the joy of doing it. The asana is a dance at the point of absolute stillness.

Incorporate some of the stretches from pages 99-101 into your daily practice, too: the child pose (see page 101) is invaluable as a rest between poses, the lying twist (see 6, page 101) is wonderful, and the cobbler's pose (see 1, page 108) gives the hips a great stretch. Do also try to integrate yoga stretches into your day: do shoulder stretches while waiting for the kettle to boil, stand on one leg while talking on the phone, put your legs up the wall for five minutes to restore flagging energy, and a quick shoulderstand (see 5, page 108) when you get home from work will make all the difference to your evening.

For the days when it is impossible to practice, you can rehearse it mentally (try this on the crowded commuter train) and amazingly it has a similar effect to actually physically doing it. This phenomenon of the brain's ability to trigger the same response from the imaginary as it does from the actual has been proved in scientific experiments. Don't strive to an external standard in your practice; relax into being yourself, and have an attitude of 'being' rather than 'doing'. Practice with *allegrezza*, with joy and intelligence.

SOME KEYS

- **Before making a movement, wait until body, breath and mind are in harmony together so that the *asana* 'happens'**
- **When we stand, the pull of gravity is from the waist down. At the same time the upper body becomes light, open, aware and relaxed**
- **When you inhale, receive, open and expand. When you exhale, allow your base to be pulled into the ground and feel the freedom in the spine**
- **All movement takes place on the out-breath. Exhalation frees the body of tension. Be passive and quiet on the in-breath**
- **Go with, not against, the body, the breath. The posture is a dance at the point of absolute stillness**
- **Don't try to 'become'. You are. The struggle of 'becoming' leads to mediocrity**
- **Don't imitate. Feel the postures. Be there. Closing the eyes can sometimes help**
- **Learn to use your right brain with its feeling, intuitive function rather than be dominated by the intellectual, judgemental function of the analytical left brain**
- **Feel, rather than think about, the stretches**

Monday

Alignment is all. Enjoy the experience of human geometry, the beauty of symmetry. Make your practice simple. Undo, relax, enjoy. Concentrate: attention is interest.

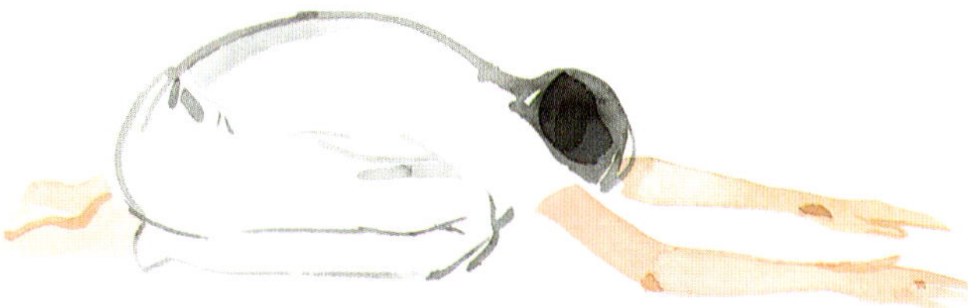

1. Sit on your heels and stretch forward with the head to the floor. Stretch the arms in front of you to open the shoulders. Relax the face and rest the eyes.

2. Kneel with hands at shoulder-width apart and toes tucked under, hip-width apart. Lift the hips and stretch the legs, heels down. Open the shoulders but keep elbows relaxed.

3. Stand in the Basic Posture (see page 91). Bend forward and, like a rag doll, relax the shoulders, neck and head. Stretch the legs, open the knees, and breathe.

4. Stand in the Basic Posture. Take one arm up behind the back as far as possible. Bring the other arm over the top and hold hands (or nearly) behind the back.

5. Lie on the floor stretched out straight, evenly balanced to either side of the spine. Drop the arms to the side, palms up, and relax the legs. Rest the eyes. Breathe.

Tuesday

Yoga comes when you do nothing. Less is more. Do not 'try', or struggle, Nothing can be achieved by force. Stay balanced, light and in alignment. Listen to your body.

1. Stand in the Basic Posture (see page 91). Bring one elbow over the other and entwine the forearms to bring palms together. Lift the forearms vertically. Breathe into the shoulders, face relaxed.

2. From the Basic Posture, step one foot forward. Keeping the weight on the back heel, stretch one arm down to the front foot with the other arm stretched up, shoulders open.

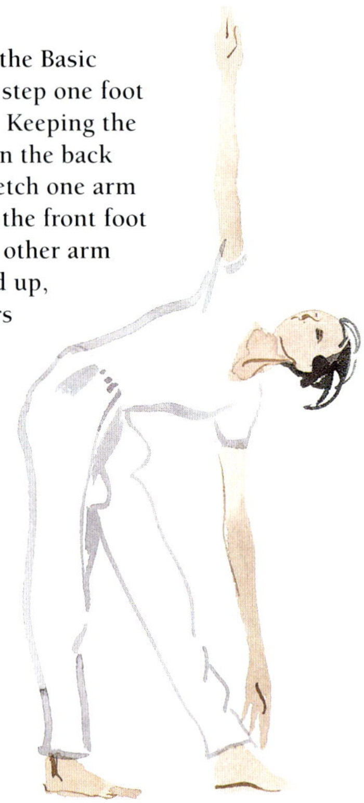

3. As 2, but bend the front knee as you come down. Keep the alignment so that the head is in line with the back hip, spine stretched, back knee open.

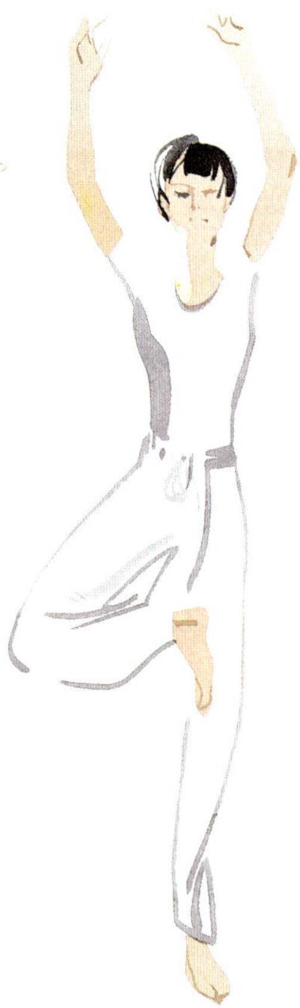

4. Stand in the Basic Posture. Take one foot up onto the opposite knee, or up into the inner thigh, knee out to the side. Bring the arms up with shoulders relaxed.

5. Stand in the Basic Posture. Place the hands in the prayer position behind the back. Step one foot forward, and stretch the trunk forward, hips back, legs straight.

Wednesday

So long as there is the shadow of ambition, you are doing the posture with the ego. Let go. Let it 'do itself'. Let go of effort, of the need to strive for results.

VARIATION FOR 2:

Take one leg up and stretch it, keeping the hips high and the other leg in line. Repeat on the other side.

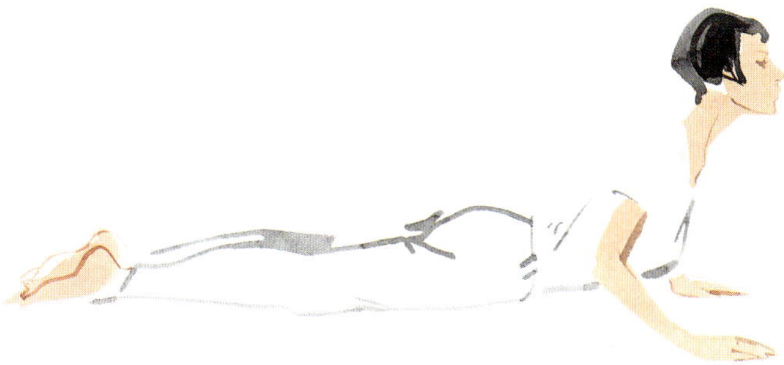

1. Lie on your front. Place the hands by the ribs and relax the shoulders. Drop the wrists into the floor and lift the trunk. Look up, and breathe, keeping hips down.

2. Lie on your back with the heels close in to the hips, toes turned in. Lift the hips keeping heels down, and support the back with your hands. Descend very slowly.

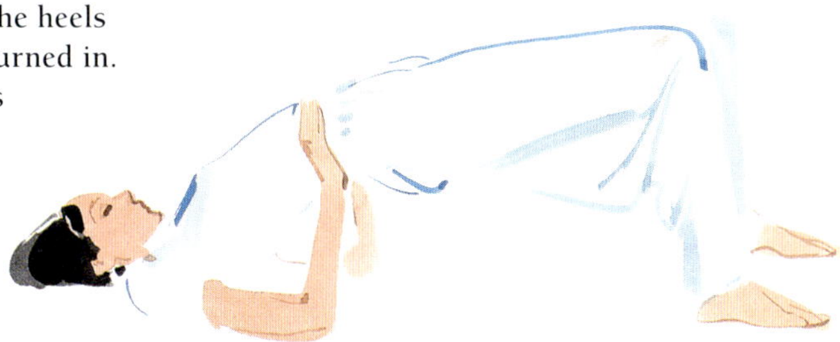

3. Kneel on one knee, the other foot forward at hip level. Take the right hand down over the left knee, turn the trunk, and hold the left hand underneath. Repeat on other side.

4. Stand in front of a stool. Take one foot up, and place the opposite hand over the knee. Turn the trunk and head keeping the hips in line. Take the other arm behind.

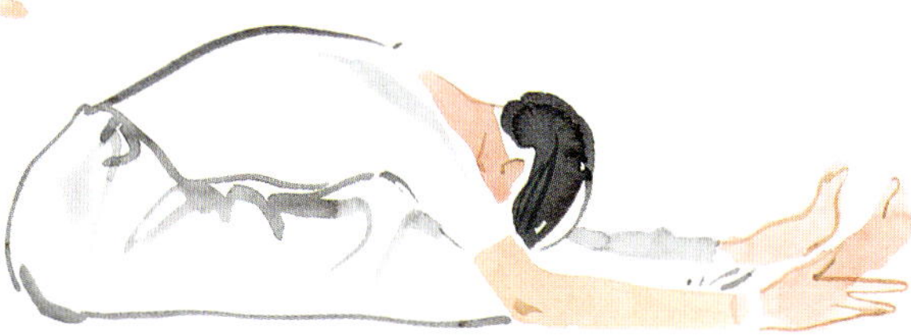

5. Sit with legs extended. Stretch forward from the hips to take hands toward the feet. Open the shoulders, relax the neck and rest the eyes. Breathe into the stretch.

Thursday

Hold a clear image of the posture and mentally undo the resistance between you and it. The correct posture is inherent in the body, but blocked by our personality/ego.

1. Sit with the soles of the feet together and stretch the spine. Place hands just above knees and ease them down towards the floor. Breathe into the stretch.

2. Lie on your back with knees close to the chest. Take arms out to shoulder level. Take the knees down towards one elbow. Turn the head and breathe.

3. Sit with one leg stretched out and the other with the heel against the groin, knee relaxed sideways. Stretch forward to take the hand towards the foot, and relax the head.

5. From 4, bring the legs up straight so that you are balancing on your shoulders. Anchor your upper arms and let the legs go up towards the ceiling. Relax.

4. Lie on your back and roll the feet over to behind the head. Support the back with the hands, keeping the elbows in. Stretch the back, open the knees, and breathe.

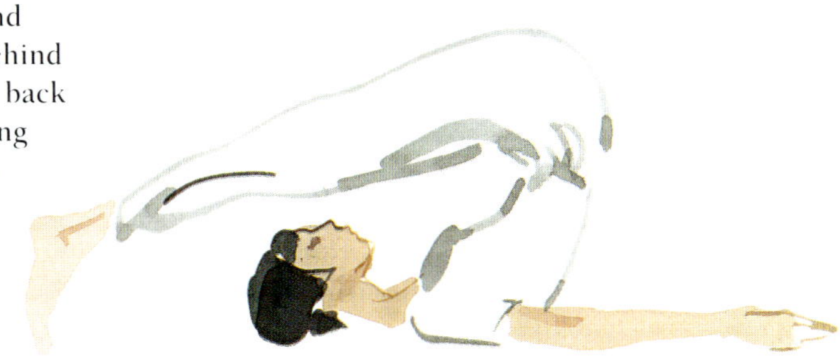

Friday

A good yoga practice combines technique with soul. Once you have learned the 'how to' with the left brain, switch to the right brain to feel the experience of the posture.

1. Kneel with the spine straight. Drop the chin to the chest and pull the head down gently. Release. Then take one ear towards one shoulder and pull the head gently. Do this on both sides.

2. Lie down and place one end of a long looped belt around the base of the skull. Place the other end around the feet. Relax back, arms out to the side.

3. Lie on your back with your feet on a bolster close to the hips. Place the soles of the feet together and drop the knees to the side. Relax the arms behind the head.

4. Sit on a bolster and place the legs over a low bed or sofa. Lie back with the bolster under the hips, and stretch the arms behind. Rest the eyes. Breathe.

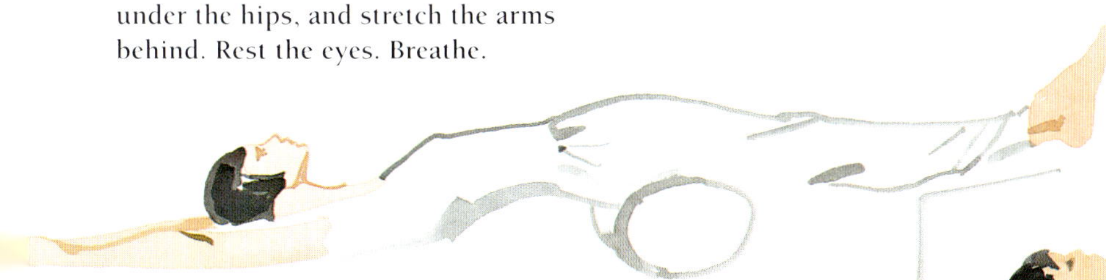

5. Sit with one hip close to the wall. Swing the body around to the floor, bringing the legs up the wall. Drop arms behind the head. Rest the eyes. Breathe.

Salute to the sun

A great way to start the day, stretching the body and deepening the breathing. Make every movement on the out-breath and keep the sequence loose and flowing. Your hips should feel free, your shoulders relaxed. Go back on the left foot first for the first side, then right foot back the second time. Repeat three times on each side.

1. Stand in the Basic Posture (see page 91), with the hands in the prayer position, thumbs against the sternum.

2. Inhale, and swing the arms back up and behind the head and arch the back.

3. Exhale, and come into a forward bend, hands to the floor. Relax the head.

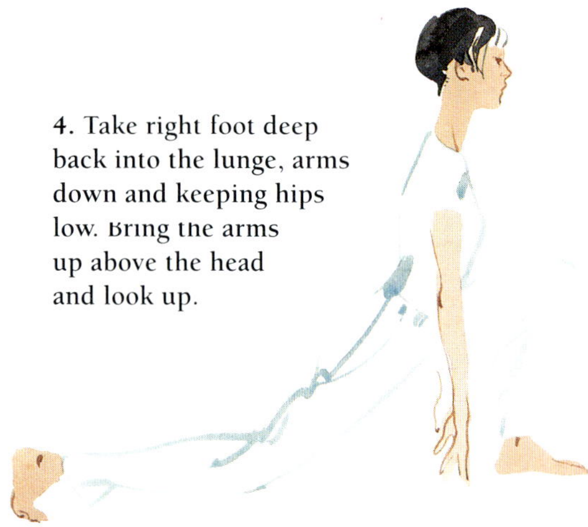

4. Take right foot deep back into the lunge, arms down and keeping hips low. Bring the arms up above the head and look up.

5. Bring both hands down to the ground and shoulder-width apart, and go into the dog pose.

6. Drop knees, chest and chin to the floor.

7. Push through into the cobra.

8. Go back into the dog pose (5).

9. Bring right foot forward into the lunge position, and bring the arms up again (4).

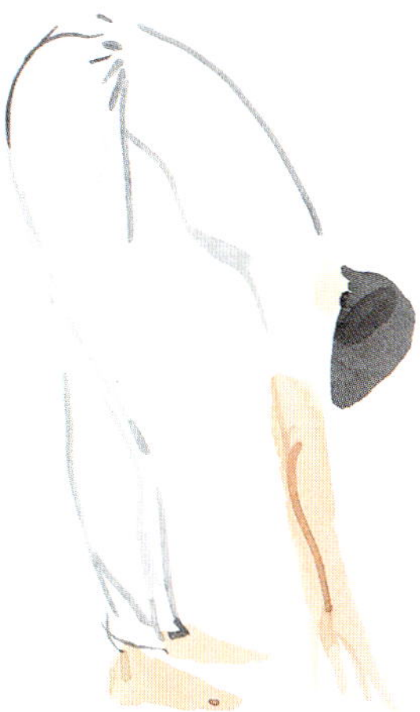

10. Step forward into the forward bend again (3).

11. Come up into the standing back arch again (2).

12. Bring the hands back to the prayer position, feet apart (1), and take a breath or two before repeating the sequence to the other side (i.e. left foot leading).

Gentle stretches for pmt and menstruation

The debilitating strain of premenstrual tension takes its toll on both energy and performance. Allowing just half an hour to do these stretches can transform you from a dish-rag into a real person again. Find a quiet space, and give your body what it needs.

1. Lie on your back with your knees towards your chest. Hold with one hand behind each knee. Relax your face and shoulders and breathe into your hips. Rest the eyes.

2. Sit with the soles of the feet together and stretch the spine. Place hands just above knees and ease them down towards the floor. Breathe into the stretch.

3. Sit with the soles of the feet together on a bolster, knees dropped apart. Lie back with a pillow under the head. Drop the arms to the side and relax the eyes.

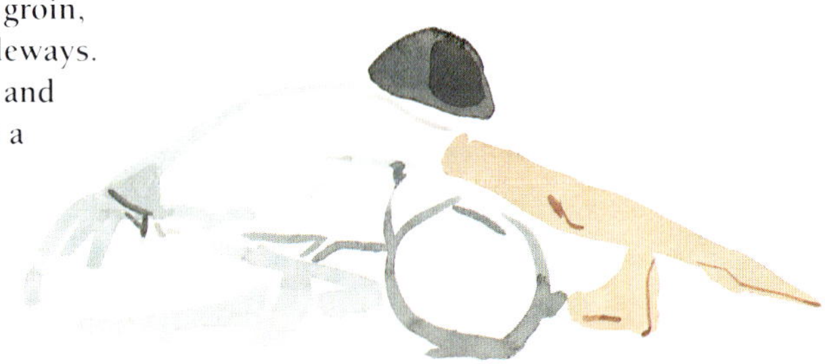

4. Sit with one leg stretched out and the other with the heel against the groin, knee relaxed sideways. Stretch forward and rest the head on a bolster, arms hanging over it.

5. Sit with one leg stretched out and the other folded back with the foot by the hip. Stretch forward, rest the head on a bolster, and relax the arms over it.

6. Sit with one leg stretched out, the other bent up with the heel by the groin. Stretch forward and rest the head on a bolster with arms hanging over it.

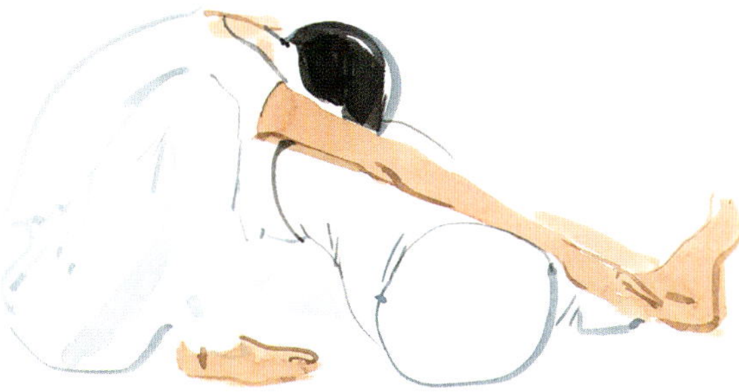

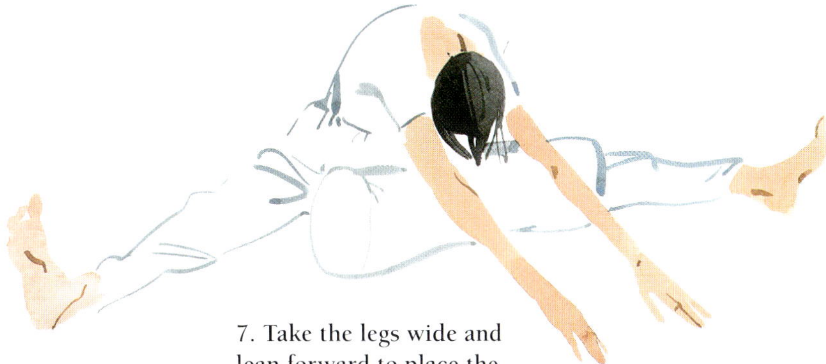

7. Take the legs wide and lean forward to place the head on a high support. Take the arms out to the side and rest the hands on each leg. Relax the eyes.

8. Sit with both legs extended. Stretch forward and rest the head on a bolster, hanging the arms over it. Rest the forehead, the eyes and the face. Follow the breath.

10. Sit with one hip close to the wall. Swing the body around to the floor, bringing the legs up the wall. Place a bolster under the hips. Drop the arms behind the head.

9. Lie back with your head on a pillow and drop the arms to the side. Rest with the soles of the feet together, knees dropping towards the floor.

Passive stretches for relaxation

Relaxation is an art. It is also a necessity to balance the stresses of a busy life. Relaxation doesn't mean becoming totally passive and 'switching off', it means becoming absorbed in an activity that you enjoy. To be effective, it has to release both physical and mental tension. These stretches, held for between five and ten minutes, achieve this. They are so comfortable that you feel as if you are doing nothing, but by the end of a session you feel deeply stretched, and released in both body and mind. Unlike the sluggish torpor of a collapse on the sofa, conscious relaxation systematically empties the mind and de-stresses the body.

The science of relaxation is measurable: it reduces blood pressure, breathing rate falls, tense muscles relax and coronary arteries dilate thus reducing the risk of chronic heart disease. It has beneficial effects on immune function, temporarily augmenting the levels of antibodies in the blood and saliva. In this, it is the direct opposite to the stress response. Anxiety and depression are relieved, and a sense of well-being results.

The brain emits beta waves in the conscious everyday state, and delta waves when we sleep. Alpha waves are slower in frequency than beta waves and indicate mild relaxation and emotional tranquillity, yet an alert mind, whereas theta waves are slower still and reflect the meditative state halfway between waking and sleeping, a dreamlike detached state. Very deep relaxation induces a predominance of alpha and theta waves in the brain, inducing a state of harmony. The combination causes biochemical changes in the brain which increase mood-enhancing neurotransmitters (brain chemicals), in particular serotonin which induces feelings of calm happiness in the body.

QUIETEN THE MIND

Wear loose, comfortable clothing and make sure that you will be warm enough, because you will not generate much of your own heat in these passive positions. In each pose, start by resting the eyes. Gently closing the eyelids, release all the muscles around the eyes, let the space between the eyebrows widen, and bring the eyes to stillness. This will help quieten the mind. Relax the jaw, release the corners of the mouth, and the tongue: more brain cells connect to the mouth than to any other part of the body apart from the hands. Relax both. Let the head drop completely into the pillow or rug so that the neck lets go. Relax through the whole body as you breathe, letting go more with each exhalation. Stay focused on following your breathing. You may find that you drop off into a light sleep in some of them – and that's OK: the more you let go, the deeper the relaxation.

FIND A QUIET PLACE

Do these long, slow stretches in a quiet, warm room where you will not be interrupted and you cannot hear the phone. For the supine stretches, place an eyebag (see page 178) over the eyes to help you relax. Have the lights down low and feel the recuperative effects of silence and solitude. The only other equipment you will need is a bolster (or tightly rolled-up blanket), a rug, and a chair or a low stool. If you have a vaporiser, burn some lavender oil to scent the room.

Follow the instructions for the stretches on page 109 (Friday's practice) and finish your session with the two postures below.

◆ Lie on your back with a bolster underneath the upper back, arms out to the side over the edge of the bolster, the head supported on a cushion. Breathe and relax.

◆ Sit with legs crossed in front of a chair. Fold the arms onto a cushion and lean forward to rest your head. Relax the forehead and rest the eyes.

Breathing techniques

When the breath wanders, or is irregular, the mind is also unsteady, but when the breath is still, so is the mind, in the words of the Hatha Yoga Pradipika, c. 1350.

Every day you take between 16,000 and 23,000 breaths. Every breath takes in 250 ml of oxygen, and disposes of 200ml carbon dioxide. In order to feel well these two need to be balanced, and you can regulate the levels of them in the bloodstream by changing the way you breathe. Shallow or irregular breathing, caused by respiratory illness, bad posture or physical tension upsets this balance, whereas fast or deep breathing causes the body to eliminate too much carbon dioxide, making the blood alkaline and cutting off carbon dioxide to the brain. Thus the art of conscious breathing is a delicate one. Indeed, in classical yoga practice *pranayama* (the control of the breath) is a skill recommended for practice only after mastering the *asanas*, when the body is tuned to itself and can move isolated muscles independently. *Prana* means both breath and life-force and consciously connects you with the energy that gives life, thereby heightening your participation in it.

Breathing is also a way of controlling the mind: it is a common experience that if you become agitated, your breath quickens; or if you are depressed and low in energy, your breathing is shallow. Conversely, if you slow the breath when you are excited, you become calmer ('take a deep breath' is commonplace advice – but it works!) Or if you up the rate of your breathing, either by taking energetic exercise or doing the Energising Breath (see page 119), then your depression will lift and you will feel more positive. The mind has responded to a change in the body's physiology, of which to some extent you are the master. So by becoming aware of, and controlling, how you breathe, you can make surprising changes in how you feel.

BREATH IS LIFE

Breathing is miraculous, each breath you breathe is life itself. No breath, no life. Breathing exercises create a bridge between the inner (body) and the outer (air). At another level, through conscious breathing the physical body becomes united with the mental and spiritual aspects of being.

The pressures of modern life restrict our breathing and for the most part we are unaware of how much. Restricting the breathing restricts your energy and your brain function. For best results practice deep breathing outside, walking or sitting in the garden, or on the beach, and make the most of fresh air: you breathe more deeply and spontaneously once you move out of doors. Then what happens is that the mind becomes clear and the body has fresh energy and better metabolism due to the increase in oxygen in the bloodstream. The nerves are soothed, resulting in evenness of mind and temper.

BREATH, THE SOURCE OF ENERGY

There are many ways of breathing: into the chest, into the back, into the abdomen, even into particular muscles. All have specific effects, highlighting the fact that breathing is the most important function of the body. It is the source of all energy, it also heals many ills. Good breathing reduces restlessness and craving. When breath is under control, the chatter of the mind quietens, and you feel at peace. If we breathe well we find abundant energy, if badly, we rob the body and brain of their full potential and vitality.

SITTING FOR BREATHING

Whichever position you choose, make sure that you are comfortable enough to sit still for several minutes. Keep the spine upright, the shoulders relaxed, and the hands resting on the thighs.

If you slump, or your chest is concave, you will immobilise your diaphragm and your breathing will be confined to the upper chest, filling only a part of your lung capacity. This puts a strain on the heart since it has to pump more blood in order to distribute the same amount of oxygen. This can also lead to increased blood pressure as the blood circulates more rapidly. Keep the eyes closed.

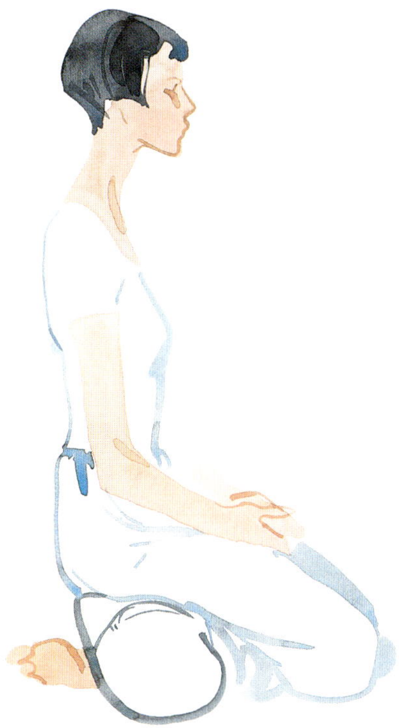

The best times to practise breathing are in the quiet of the early morning, or after sunset.

BASIC DEEP BREATHING

Simple deep breathing boosts your energy, helps your digestive system, clears the mind and soothes away stress. But never force the breath, and stop if you feel dizzy.

DEEP ABDOMINAL BREATHING

This is a useful practice which, once you have mastered it, you can do either sitting, walking or standing.

- **Sit in a comfortable position with your hands resting on your knees and the shoulders relaxed**
- **Exhale completely through your mouth, allowing the chest to deflate and the abdomen to drop back**
- **Inhale slowly through the nose, allowing the abdomen to rise and swell, but keeping the chest and shoulders still. The belly moves out on the inhalation, and drops back in on the exhalation**
- **Once you get into the practice you can mentally say to yourself 'calm – in' as you breathe in, and 'tension – out' as you breathe out**
- **Repeat ten to fifteen times**

THE KUMBHAKA BREATH

The practice of *kumbhaka* in *pranayama* is of retaining the breath on the inhalation, and of restraining the breath on the exhalation. In practice it is important to hold the breath without effort or strain, but rather to simply suspend breathing for a short interval, keeping relaxed as you do so. The Sanskrit word means a water jug or pitcher, and the idea is that you fill the container (your lungs, effectively your upper body) on the inhalation, and empty it completely on the exhalation.

Sit comfortably in an upright but relaxed position, either in a chair (see page 93), kneeling (see page 117) or cross-legged (see opposite). Breathe in deeply but softly and fill your lungs right to the brim. Suspend the breathing for a few seconds. Then slowly empty the body of breath, and when you have exhaled fully, suspend breathing again to restrain the in-breath for a few seconds. Enjoy the stillness.

Remember that you are taking in not just air when you breathe in, but *prana*, life-force: you are vitalising the whole body (and mind) with this practice. When you breathe out, you are breathing out waste in the form of carbon dioxide, but also releasing tension and negativity from the body.

BREATHING TO DE-STRESS

Lie flat on your back and relax. If your lower back is uncomfortable in this position, lie with the knees bent and feet on the floor. Place your hands on the belly. Slowly inhale and exhale through your nose. Don't try consciously to move your abdomen or chest but just let the hands pick up the gentle movement of the breath as it moves through the body. Let go as you exhale, as if sighing or yawning. After a while, still keeping the breathing relaxed, deepen the breath and move the hands to the ribs to feel the movement there. Stage three is to take a deep in-breath, fill the lungs to capacity and hold for a few seconds. Then purse your lips and slowly blow out the air on a long, deep exhalation. Pause for ten seconds, then repeat the whole cycle. Do this up to ten times, morning and evening.

BREATHING AWAY ANXIETY

You can lie or sit. Close the eyes and relax the face. Keep the shoulders relaxed.

- **Breathe in for a count of four**
- **Hold the breath for a count of four**
- **Exhale slowly on a count of four**

You can increase the count to six, then to eight, but always stop if you feel dizzy. Practise this for four to five minutes, then return to normal breathing.

COUNTING THE BREATH

If you want to develop a regular breathing practice to calm yourself, quieten your mind and relax your body.

Sit comfortably (see opposite). Close the eyes and relax the face. Breathe normally for a few moments, following the breath and become aware of its movement in the body. Then start to count: at the end of each out-breath, one, then two, and so on up to ten. If your mind wanders and you lose count, start back at one again. When you get to ten, start back at one.

You can also try counting on the in-breath. Because of the concentration involved in this practice, the mind is stilled and doesn't get a chance to play its tricks: the monkey-mind is outwitted.

Alternatively, count backwards from fifty to zero, synchronising the breath with the count, even numbers on the exhalation, odd numbers on the inhalation. From twenty downwards, count only on the exhalation.

ENERGISING BREATH

This is a fast pumping action which clears stale air from the bottom of the lungs and pumps oxygen into the bloodstream. This breath produces alpha waves in the brain and increases oxygen levels in the bloodstream. You feel energized but calm and clear-headed after this practice.

Sit upright and relaxed. Breathe very rapidly through your nostrils at a rate of about one exhalation per second, with no pause between the in-breath and the out-breath. You will feel your abdomen pulling back sharply on the exhalation (you can exaggerate this). Do this for up to forty breaths only, and pause to breathe normally for a few moments. Gradually you can build the practice up to sixty. Stop if you feel light-headed.

ALTERNATE NOSTRIL BREATH

This breath balances the energies between the right and left sides of the body (brain) and leaves you feeling tranquil and clear-headed.

Sit in a relaxed and upright position (see illustration) Close and rest the eyes. Place the index and middle fingers between the eyebrows and place the right thumb on the right side of the nose just above the nasal bone in the little dent above the nostril. Your ring finger will be used to close the left nostril in the same area of the nose.

Start by inhaling through both nostrils, then close the left nostril and exhale and inhale through the right. Close the right nostril, open the left and exhale and inhale through the left. Continue this practice keeping the breathing relaxed and smooth and deep. Finish by exhaling though the left nostril, after four to five minutes. Remain with eyes closed and watch the breath as it returns to normal.

Always do your breathing practices on an empty stomach, never immediately after a meal since your body will be working overtime on digestive processes and won't be able to cope effectively with the powerful effects of *pranayama* at the same time.

While you are practising breathing you should feel no strain at all in the face, eyes or neck, and be able to sit upright but still feel relaxed.

Eating well, naturally

Don't diet

The word diet has acquired a terrible meaning during the latter decades of the 20th century, becoming synonymous with extreme control. A fashion for thinness bordering on emaciation has induced a culture of self-hatred which affects the mind and spirit too. But the word 'diet' actually means 'way of living', from the Latin meaning 'day'. It's as much about what as how and why we eat, every day. Diet implies balance, and a 'natural' diet implies finding out what suits our body, at the weight that feels good for us and which gives us vitality, energy and self-esteem.

The stomach is the seat of all wisdom
CHINESE PROVERB

***Food is wonderful. It is one of the miracles of daily life, and the alchemy of cooking is one of the great human expressions of love and communion. The word 'companion' means 'breaking bread together'. As a social barometer, food is status, honour, a symbol of worth. Food is powerful. 'One cannot think well, sleep well, love well if one has not dined well', says Virginia Woolf in* A Room of One's Own.**

There is a genetic factor in body weight which is a constant factor and which you cannot change without damaging yourself. A well balanced, natural diet entails taking responsibility for our own body, not comparing it with anyone else's, but becoming aware of its unique needs and how these needs change over successive eras of life. No woman's body is the same as another and all bodies have their own unique, special beauty. Thinking positively about your body, and thinking lucidly about what you are putting into it, how much, and why, becomes a habit, a way of life.

The fashion for dieting has distorted personal body image to such an extent that a staggeringly high percentage of women want, more than anything in life (love, pleasure, enlightenment, success...), to lose some weight! This even applies to women who are not overweight. A recent survey showed that 67 per cent of women are unhappy about their shape, and 77 per cent had dieted at some time or other. No busy woman can function fully on a strict calorie-controlled diet because hungry humans obsess on food to the exclusion of all else. Japanese prisoners of war had long conversations about menus and dinner parties, endlessly dreaming of food between minuscule rations of prison gruel. There is no room left for being creative, motivated, successful, energetic, expressive, having fun and exploring life if you are starving. Self-esteem and effectiveness are weakened, depression and irritability set in, and passivity takes over. The joy of natural energy is overridden by the growling stomach. A poor diet raises blood pressure, damaging cognitive function, disrupting memory and concentration. It affects your mood, your behaviour and the way you think. Poor diet also has a marked effect on immune function.

Dieting is unnatural. It not only makes tens of thousands of women (mostly) seriously unwell, it can also have the opposite effect to the desired one. It so confuses the body's regulatory mechanisms that its metabolism becomes disturbed. Dieting makes you fat. Metabolic rate declines and any temporary weight loss is followed by

rapid gain. Although caloric restriction leads to loss of weight, it is accompanied by greater loss of protein or lean tissue. Conversely weight-loss through exercise maximizes the removal of fat and minimizes loss of protein, helping maintain metabolic rate. The muscles in your body burn more calories than any other tissue, so the more muscular you are, the more calories you burn.

Dieting for weight control is on record as an unsuccessful method: only 10 per cent of people who have lost 55kg (25 lbs) or more will remain at their desired weight. So rather than crash dieting to shed extra kilos, eat R.E.A.L food (see page 129), following food combining principles and incorporating both sattvic and superfoods (see pages 136-137), for lifelong stability of body weight.

Modern research shows the powerful connection between good nutrition and optimum brain function. Food is important.

Natural foods

Eating a natural, balanced diet is actually one of the most important things we can do for ourselves. It affects our health, our well-being, our whole life. It is primary. 'You are what you eat' is a truism found in many cultures. It is nothing less than astonishing how unaware many of us are of what we are putting into our bodies. Raising your awareness of exactly what you are eating will have a huge effect on not only your body but on your mental functioning and emotional life too.

It's not as if we cannot know: contemporary food labelling is detailed, and much has been talked about in the media about additives, preservatives, fertilizers, hormones, genetic engineering and all the other aids to modern food production. These processes go against nature; but nature always kicks back. We get ill if we eat tampered substances, with food poisoning, salmonella and e-coli. Or slowly but dramatically we die if we turn cattle – gentle vegetarians – into cannibals. BSE has shown that humans must not change the laws of nature. Quite possibly the effect of genetically modified foods will be the next terrible lesson to teach us not to meddle with nature.

WHAT ARE WE EATING?

Reclaiming a natural way of eating is in fact very simple. Just avoid eating processed and pre-packaged foods and turn instead to a diet of fresh, organically produced foods.

Many of the fruits and vegetables on the supermarket shelf have been sprayed up to eighteen times. Fruits may be waxed with animal- or insect-based resins to maintain 'freshness', potatoes sprayed with toxic fungicides after harvest to stop them sprouting, and tomatoes treated with ionizing radiation, let alone what goes on to them while they are growing. Organo-phosphates, insecticides, aldicarb pesticides, methyl bromide… the list goes on. Do we really want to be eating this stuff? Giving it to our children? Poisoning our bodies with so-called 'fresh' produce? We must insist on knowing how our food has been treated before we put it into our bodies, and the trend for meals in the new millennium should be increasingly organic.

GO ORGANIC

'Natural' means, in today's world, 'organic': it has to. More and more people are becoming concerned with obtaining organic food, and even though it may cost a little more, it contains less water and more solid matter and nutrients – so you are getting your money's-worth. Organic foodstuffs are grown on land which has been free from artificial fertilizers and pesticidal chemicals for at least five years (although there is a 'conversion' grade acceptable after two), using instead natural manures and pest controls.

Intensive farming has devastated the topsoil and bleached it of all-important minerals: it is essential to redress the balance of nature, and we can all do our bit by supporting the organic movement. There are delivery services (see page 205), and a sprinkling of organic restaurants. The major supermarkets sell organic foodstuffs in growing volumes and at increasingly low cost – one high-street chainstore actually pledged to sell organic fruits and vegetables at standard prices, and increased their sales by 100 per cent over the course of one year alone.

Women are recognising that they are far more likely to achieve optimum health and vitality if they are *not* ingesting toxic material. Clearly, healthy eaters not only live longer, they live their lives feeling better. And, the big bonus, organic food tastes so much better. Eat well, and save the planet at the same time.

The ethos of producing quality, healthy food while protecting and enhancing the environment and caring for the countryside, is based on working with natural systems which sustain soil fertility and minimise pollution.

Organic farming helps preserve and enhance wildlife habitats, and it respects animal welfare at all levels, thus protecting biodiversity as well as the beauty and natural balance of the countryside.

Fast food

Fast food is almost always junk food. It *is* junk. It is empty of nutrients, packed with nasties like fats, sugars and salt, a heady cocktail of preservatives, additives, and ghastly flavour-enhancers. It is not good for your body or your brain. You wouldn't run a sports car on rubbish fuel so why do that to your own body? To be fair, fast food has a place because we lead busy lives. But let it be healthy food. Commercial fast food is not natural food, it is usually highly processed and contains hidden horrors. It is extremely unlikely to be organic. All in all, it is a false economy. This doesn't mean that you *never* touch it: it's a question of balance, of moderation. The occasional pizza or burger is not going to kill you. But if it is daily fare, beware. Don't fuel with fast food, use R.E.A.L food instead (see page 129).

Fast food bypasses not only the nutrition factor but also the therapeutic and comforting element of home-cooking. It would be tragic if real cooking became a mere spectator sport as we watch celebrities doing their thing on TV. If you are truly too exhausted to cook at the end of the day, you can fix great, nutritious salads in no time at all, and feel vital and radiant at the end of the meal instead of heavy and full. Stock the fridge with a variety of fresh organic vegetables including all the salads, and you can fix a beautiful meal quite quickly. Eat lots of raw food: it's filling as well as nourishing. Alternatively, just cook extremely simply: a stir-fry of fresh crisp vegetables with coriander and ginger, or steamed broccoli with garlic and chilli, or noodle and pasta dishes – these take next to no time at all to prepare and make satisfying meals. And then when you do have time and energy, and are in the mood for a session in the kitchen, cook in quantity and freeze meal-size batches. Insist on good food, rather than fast food.

If you are hungry between meals have a piece of fruit – fresh or dried – or a raw carrot, some nuts or seeds. Plain yoghurt is a wonderful filler and provides helpful bacteria for the gut which aid digestion. When you hit that late afternoon slump, diving for the chocolate bar is an unhealthy habit which is hard to break. If you don't keep biscuits and salted snacks in the house or office you won't succumb to their dangerous temptations at peckish moments. Savoury snacks are very seductive but they are high in fats as well as salt – negative addictions that are lethal for the waistline. If you are one of those people who prefer to eat little and often, make sure that the little is made up of healthy food! And even when you are under great pressure and have only a little time for a meal, give your food your full attention, enjoy its flavours, appreciate its smell and celebrate it in even the smallest way.

Being mindful of the amazing gift of food, the miraculous processes which transform it from seed to plant, its metamorphosis into food via alchemical and manual skills, is part of the richness of the ritual of eating.

Foods that are especially good for brain function are shellfish, sardines, herrings and pilchards; dried and sprouted beans, seeds and nuts, apricots, apples and blackcurrants, beetroot, carrots and celery, oats, brown rice, molasses and liquorice.

The protein myth is indeed just that – if you are eating a daily combination of wholegrain cereals, vegetables, low fat dairy products, nuts, seeds and fruits and beans, you will be getting all you need, and in abundance.

R.E.A.L. food

This simple formula is not regulated by complicated rules but is a way of eating which is easy to remember and possible to incorporate into a busy life. It's satisfying, it's sociable, it stimulates the brain and keeps the body healthy. It meets the nutritional needs of women who are leading busy, active lives. Just remember, get R.E.A.L.

R is for REGULAR MEALS
Eating well-balanced meals at regular intervals prevents blood sugar falling to low levels: if it does, you don't function well either physically or mentally. The brain needs a regular supply of glucose and oxygen, so regular consumption of balanced and varied meals provides a steady and even conversion of food into glucose, plus adequate amounts of iron to ensure oxygen-carrying ability in the blood. 'Little and often' is a useful rule, it maintains energy levels and keeps cholesterol down.

E is for EAT A BALANCED DIET
Eating a balanced and varied diet improves the biochemical functioning of the brain and this above all is what busy women need. The R.E.A.L. diet is food for the brain, it provides a wide variety of foods which supply instant energy (natural sugars), plus some that give slower release (complex carbohydrates) and then those that take a long time to break down (proteins). This balanced diet is low in saturated fats, sugar and salt, and has plenty of fresh vegetables and fruits, raw and cooked. Pulses or fish provide protein, unrefined carbohydrates the high octane fuel.

A is for AVOID PROCESSED FOODS
at all costs. They have been substantially changed from their natural state and have hefty doses of fat, sugar and salt cunningly concealed with additives and artificial flavourings straight from the laboratory. Food processing aids include the use of enzymes, propellants, solvents and added oils, none of which are on the label. These products may be irradiated, genetically modified or treated with a take-your-pick selection of growth hormones, antibiotics, flavour-enhancers, E-numbers, fungicides, emulsifiers, stabilizers and other mystery ingredients not all of which legally have to be declared.

L is for LIGHT AND LOW
Low in fat and light on the calories is the final premise of the R.E.A.L. diet. Low in fat is good for the brain and good for the body because the blood does not circulate so efficiently when it is full of fat. Fat rots your brain. Forget the fried bacon for breakfast, the hamburger for lunch and that juicy steak in the evening. Keeping your daily fat levels to between 25-30 per cent of your intake will give you all the fuel you need for an active and healthy lifestyle.

Processed foods, like breakfast cereals, most packaged foods and pre-cooked meals, and even bread, are high in hidden sugar and salt. Not so with nutrient-dense foods which are natural and have not been tampered with. A bodily system struggling with high intakes of sugar and salt is not likely to cope well at high levels of pressure.

One-third of your daily intake should consist of raw, fresh salads, fruit and vegetables which your body requires for optimum performance. Their beneficial 'side-effects' are being increasingly evaluated by food-scientists: for example, a diet high in vegetables and vitamins reduces the symptoms of PMS to a marked degree, people who eat fresh fruit every day are less like to die of strokes and heart attacks, and some vegetables have been found to contain anti-carcinogens.

Eat light: keeping to a relatively low-calorie diet, around 1500-2000 per day for physically active working women makes you feel good, vital, and full of energy. It has been shown that people who live on fewer calories live longer. Too much food can block your energy, the wrong food can, as we have seen, pollute body and brain. You will feel better and fresher on a relatively light diet which gives you all the nutrients you need for optimum function without the drag of carting excess flab around with you. Make sure that the foods are nutrient dense (this is where organic fruits and vegetables and salads score so heavily). Fifty per cent of your diet should be made up of a wide variety of grains and seeds, 30 per cent fruits and vegetables, and the rest dairy, fish and a little lean meat if you insist on including in in your diet. Following the R.E.A.L. diet guidelines (see below) will equip you for a busy but balanced life.

The R.E.A.L food pyramid

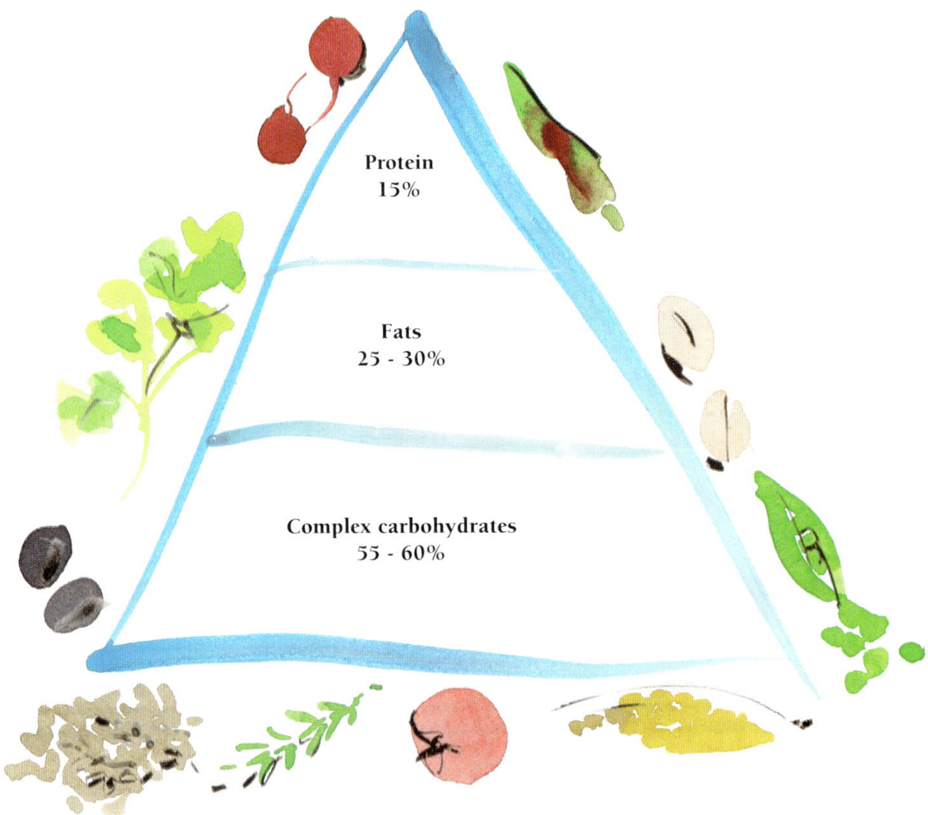

A typical day on R.E.A.L. food

This is close to the Mediterranean diet so widely accepted as the healthiest and most balanced way of eating in the west. It provides daily complex carbohydrates, fruit, vegetables, olive oil, and yogurt. A few times a week fish, eggs and sweet dishes are included, and for people who want it, lean meat can feature occasionally each month. Along with a moderate intake of wine and regular physical activity, it will keep you in perfect health.

Keep breakfast high in protein, low in fat and with only a little carbohydrate otherwise you will feel sleepy again immediately afterwards. Never skip breakfast: it restores glucose levels and enhances learning, memory and thinking.

BREAKFAST

Masses of fresh fruit, making it into a fruit salad if you have time

or… low fat live yogurt with some toasted almonds sprinkled over, plus poached egg with baked beans or grilled tomatoes

MID-MORNING

Snack of dried unsulphured apricots, raisins, dates or fresh nuts

LUNCH

Fish or low-fat cheese with a large mixed salad. Add sunflower, sesame or pumpkin seeds to it and include plenty of watercress and tomatoes

or… a miso-based Japanese soup with tofu, seaweed and vegetables, served with rice crackers

MID-AFTERNOON

Apple, pear, small bunch of grapes

EVENING MEAL

A stir-fry of mixed vegetables with rice, noodles or quinoa

or… any tasty vegetarian main course dish relatively low in fat

or… a root-vegetable casserole with potato, turnips. carrots, onions, celery, beetroot, kidney or cannellini beans, and rice or barley. Lots of salad.

or… a salad meal with some fresh wholemeal bread

DURING THE EVENING

Banana, a few dried figs or dates, or a mix of seeds and nuts

or… some low-fat plain yogurt

Food combining

Incorporating food combining into the R.E.A.L. diet is simple once you've got your head around it: all you need is to be awake to what you are eating. The Hay diet has long-term success in its favour: it was formulated in the early part of the 20th century by the American pioneer Dr. William Hay who cured his own severe ill-health by eating according to what he saw as natural laws. A book explaining the Hay system (see *Bookshelf* page 204) is still a best-seller and huge numbers of people have found that it is the only 'diet' that works in the long term, both for health, for weight regulation and for energy. Its essence is 'don't mix foods that fight.'

EATING OUT
If you are invited to someone's house for a meal, let them know what you don't eat. It is more than rude to refuse someone's food, whatever your scruples, because they have prepared it for you, and your rejection is more than of the food itself. Unless you are prepared to eat anything that is put in front of you, it is best to make your situation clear from the beginning, for everyone's sake.

THE HAY PRINCIPLES

- **Starch and sugar should not be eaten with proteins and acid fruits**
- **Salads, vegetables and fruit should form the major part of the diet**
- **Proteins, starches and fats to be eaten in small quantities**
- **No processed foods, especially white flour**
- **Leave about four hours between meals of different character**
- **Desert the dessert (most of the time). Refined sugars are not useful**

The chart opposite, based on Dr. Hay's work in nutrition, is a straightforward guideline: and it really works. It gives energy and stamina, you are never starving hungry and therefore listless, and the digestive system functions at optimum level. He divides foods into proteins, starches and neutral foods – which can be eaten with either of the other two groups. Fruit is a neutral food, considered the most important part of the diet to be eaten, ideally, at every meal. Dr. Hay recommends a good fruit breakfast and this is a fabulous way to start the day, especially in summer when you can fill your bowl with peaches, nectarines, figs, raspberries, grapes, mangoes and other wonderful fruits of the earth.

A protein lunch works really well because protein is digested slowly over a long period of time and does not put the instant demands on the system that a carbohydrate meal does, therefore avoiding feelings of sleepiness in early afternoon. It's useful to remember that if you have an important meeting in the afternoon and you want be be fully alert and focused, then forego the starches and animal fats at lunchtime. Save them for later. A carbohydrate-based meal in the evening is conducive to relaxing as you wind down after a day's work. Remembering not to combine starches with proteins may be hard at first, but following the guide closely for the first few weeks will soon break old habits. People who follow this way of eating find it gives them high energy levels, they have no digestive problems and their minds feel clear and sharp.

A guide to compatible foods

1 and 2 can be combined, 2 and 3 can be combined, 1 and 3 *cannot* be combined

1. FOODS FOR PROTEIN MEALS
can include:

Protein
any kind of meat, poultry and game, all fish and shellfish, eggs, cheese, yogurt

Fruit
apples, fresh and dried apricots, blackberries, blueberries, cherries black, red or whitecurrants, gooseberries, grapefruit, grapes, kiwis, lemons, limes, mangoes, melons (the only fruit that should be eaten alone), nectarines, oranges, papayas, pears, pineapples, raspberries, satsumas, strawberries, tangerines

Salad dressings
vinaigrette (using either lemon juice or cider vinegar), home-made mayonnaise, a simple cream dressing

Alcohol
dry white or red wine, dry cider

NB
Milk combines best with fruit and should not be part of a meat meal

Melons are best eaten alone, as a fruit meal

Pulses are not recommended by Dr. Hay as they are too high in both starch and protein; but vegetarians may use them

2. NEUTRAL FOODS
(to go with either protein or starch meals) can include:

Fats
butter, cream, egg yolks, virgin olive oil, preferably cold-pressed and organic sunflower or sesame oil

Vegetables
can include all green and root vegetables *except* potatoes and Jerusalem artichokes, e.g. asparagus, aubergines, beetroot, leeks, broccoli, brussels sprouts, cabbage, calabrese, onions, carrots, cauliflower, celery, celeriac, courgettes, green beans, kohlrabi, turnips marrow, mushrooms, peas, parsnips, spinach, swedes

Salads
avocados, chicory, cucumber, fennel, garlic, all fresh green herbs, lettuce, mustard, cress, peppers, radishes, spring onions, sprouted seeds, tomatoes, watercress, (orange and lemon rind for salad dressings

Nuts and Seeds
all nuts apart from peanuts (they are legumes and difficult to digest), sunflower, sesame and pumpkin seeds

Bran
wheat or oat bran wheatgerm

Alcohol
whisky, gin

3. FOODS FOR STARCH MEALS
can include:

Cereals
wholegrain wheat, barley, sweetcorn, oats, millet, rice and rye, wholewheat bread, flour-based foods (wholewheat preferably) e.g. pasta, medium oatmeal

milk and yogurt
in strict moderation

Sweet fruits
ripe bananas, dates, fresh and dried figs, sweet grapes, ripe papaya, ripe pears, currants, raisins and sultanas

Vegetables
potatoes, Jerusalem artichokes

Salad dressings
cream or soured cream, olive oil, cold-pressed seed oils, fresh tomato juice

Alcohol
beer or ale

Sugars
dark brown sugar (scant amounts), moderate amounts of honey

Sugar Subsitutes
For protein meals – use frozen orange juice
For starch meals – use raisins, honey or maple syrup, in moderation

The wonder of water

Herb teas are one delicious way of taking in regular liquid – fennel is my favourite, and lemon verbena is bliss.

Caffeine increases irritability, nervousness and insomnia, and has the rebound effect of lethargy and fatigue.

What we drink has an enormous effect on our bodies and brains. I used to drink black coffee endlessly and I have always loved good wine. As my body became more sensitive to the effects of caffeine and alcohol I have regulated my intake and feel far better for it. I hardly ever drink caffeinated coffee now, but enjoy delicious organic coffee decaffeinated without chemicals. Although caffeine enhances mood, improves cognition and memory and heightens visual perception, too much of it is over-stimulating and counter-productive. It increases the output of adrenalin and can become addictive at the expense of your own natural energy.

We often confuse thirst with hunger – both are controlled by the hypothalamus – and frequently water will disperse these so-called 'hunger' pangs. The recommended quantity of water per day is between 1½ to 3 litres. Not drinking enough water can dehydrate muscle over the long term and lead to chronic problems including even low back pain. Your skin wrinkles faster if you are de-hydrated, and the gut becomes blocked to cause piles and constipation.

Our bodies are made up of two-thirds water so it is our most important nutrient: we lose as much as 1½ litres per day through the skin and through urine, and it has to be replaced. Bad breath in the morning is a result of, among other things, not drinking enough liquid, which causes bacteria to form in the mouth. Also, water gives you strength: I have never forgotten watching a kinesiologist doing a diagnostic test on my son where he asked him to put out his arm and resist pressure on it. The doctor pressed down hard and Nick's arm flopped. He gave him a glass of water, did the same thing, and the arm had the strength to resist the same pressure. Think of a glass of water as a source of energy.

Packaged fruit juices which are high in acids can damage the teeth. Don't waste your time on canned drinks either normal or light – they are empty of nutrients and high in sugar or sweeteners, additives and preservatives. It's fair enough to enjoy a glass of wine to relax in the evening with friends or family, but if you drink alcohol in any quantity, make sure that you match it with the same of water to flush out undesired after-effects of over-indulgence.

I drink masses of water every day and I am convinced that this is what keeps my skin clear: it cleans out the system, flushing out toxins and impurities. I like to collect beautiful glasses and I drink my water from a favourite which is tinted blue and gives its cool colour to the liquid it contains.

The yogic way of eating

It is interesting that what the Indian Vedic scriptures of about 1500 B.C. had to say about food for body and soul is still applicable today. Just as with the philosophical wisdom of yoga and the bodywork, this advice does not seem to age: it works. What we eat plays an integral part in the development of our inner nature because it is intrinsic to body-mind balance. The yogic philosophy sees all energy in the universe as having three qualities: inertia or darkness (*tamas*), activity or passion and the process of change (*rajas*), and purity (*sattva*). The three qualities (they are called *gunas*) are present in all substances, but also certain foods come under each heading.

TAMAS
INERTIA
That food which is stale, putrid, rotten and impure refuse, is the food liked by the Tamasic.

RAJAS
OVERACTIVITY
The foods that are bitter, sour, saline, excessively hot, pungent, dry and burning, are liked by the Rajasic and are productive of pain grief and disease.

SATTVA
PURITY
The foods which increase life, purity, strength, health, joy and cheerfulness, which are savoury and oleaginous, substantial and agreeable, are dear to the sattva people.
BHAGAVAD GITA

TAMASIC FOODS

meat, fish, eggs, alcohol, drugs, overcooked and packaged foods, fermented foods such as vinegar, burned and barbecued foods, fried food, stale and overripe foods and reheated foods

Tamasic foods produce feelings of heaviness and lethargy and benefit neither body nor mind. They make you feel dull and lazy and undermine your purpose and motivation, and even your high ideals. People who eat too much tamasic food often suffer from chronic ailments and depression, their powers of reasoning can be affected and their immune system depleted. Tamasic foods make people angry and greedy. Overeating is regarded as tamasic.

RAJASIC FOODS

onions, garlic, tea, coffee, tobacco, highly spiced and salted foods, many ready-prepared convenience foods and snacks, refined sugar, soft drinks, chocolate

Rajasic foods disturb the sensitive mind-body equilibrium by feeding the body at the expense of the mind. They overstimulate and excite making the mind restless and uncontrollable. Physical restlessness and overactivity ensue, and the equilibrium of body and mind that is essential for inner peace is thereby destroyed. People who eat too much rajasic food are often physically and mentally stressed. They may also suffer circulatory and nervous disorders. Eating in a hurry is considered rajasic.

SATTVIC FOODS

fresh and dried fruits and berries, pure fruit juices, raw or lightly cooked vegetables , salads, grains, legumes, nuts, seeds, wholemeal bread, honey, fresh herbs, herbal teas, spring water, milk, butter and cheese, cereals, no additives

Sattvic foods calm the mind and sharpen the intellect. They are easy to digest and supply optimum energy to the body. Endurance and stamina are improved and people who eat sattvic food do not suffer as much from fatigue. Food which is soothing and nourishing to the body brings calmness and purity to the mind. People who eat sattvic foods tend to be cheerful and serene, clear-headed and lithe of body. With mental poise goes an equilibrium of the nervous system.

A sattvic diet of natural, unprocessed foods results in a peaceful mind in control of a fit body, with a balanced flow of energy between the two – one of the best tools for dealing with the stresses and demands of everyday life. It is a simple way of eating, inclusive and easy to remember, and provides the energy and balance you need for a busy working and family life.

This way of eating will stand you in good stead over the years. This is not to say that you must stick to it to the letter: certainly I put rajasic spices and garlic into my dishes – they are an essential part of good cooking – but who is to say that it isn't altogether a bad thing to stir up a little activity! Likewise a glass of wine to relax with at the end of the day may be tamasic but it is relaxing and good for the soul.

The yogic philosophy also offers guidelines of *how* to eat. It recommends keeping to regular mealtimes, but not eating if you are not hungry – in which case fast until the next mealtime. And never eat when you are angry or upset. Always sit down to eat, and sit quietly for a few minutes afterwards. Eat slowly and savour the food, chewing it thoroughly. Eat simply – don't confuse and overload the digestive system by mixing too many foods at the same meal, and follow the food combining principles whenever you can. Always eat at least one raw salad per day.

The culture of overeating has spread like a disease through the affluent world, but rather than filling your face with large quantities, go for quality: feel satisfied, not stuffed! Just half-fill the stomach with food, fill another quarter with liquid and leave the rest with space enough for the gases to move and the digestive processes to work with ease. This will make you feel fresher and give you much more energy after the meal.

Purity of mind depends on purity of food
Swami Sivananda

Superfoods

Quantities of dark green leafy vegetables protect us from cancer among many other diseases: Cato said of the cabbage that it had allowed the Roman nation to survive for six hundred years without any doctors.

Particular foods act in particular ways on the body and you can balance your own health-needs using food as medicine. Not only will eating well, 'naturally' and in tune with your body, enhance your overall mental and physical ability and performance, it will shield you from illness. Furthermore one of the most potent activators of the immune system is a relaxed and happy mind, and eating well has a built-in feel-good factor. Make sure that you get regular amounts of the following foods (the quantities will depend on your age and lifestyle). Stock up with them so that they become a feature of your weekly diet. They all contain valuable proteins, vitamins and minerals, they boost the immune system, fight infection and keep the body in balance. For more information refer to 'Foods for Body and Mind' (see *Bookshelf* page 204).

APPLES

Beneficial for arthritis and generally maintaining good health, apples also detoxify and lower cholesterol

APRICOTS

Dried unsulphured are good for skin, constipation, high blood pressure, fluid retention and anaemia

BEETROOT

Raw beetroot juice is an unrivalled source of minerals and vitamins and is a renowned blood-cleanser and tonic

CABBAGE

One of nature's panaceas, according to wisdom both ancient and modern, cabbage contains healing substances. Eating any of the brassicas three times per week can reduce the risk of colon cancer by 60 per cent

CARROTS

One of the great superfoods, an anti-cancer food which has countless other effects too. Eat organic whenever possible. One carrot gives you your entire vitamin A requirement for one day, and is excellent for eyesight

GARLIC

The king of the healing plants: used from very ancient times and still recognised as such today.

Naturally antibacterial, antifungal and antiviral, it combats cancer, heart problems and major infections

OLIVE OIL

Rich in antidioxants, olive oil protects the heart from cardiovascular disease, and helps keep cholesterol low

ONIONS

Eating just half an onion per day keeps your cholesterol down! Onions benefit heart and circulation, anaemia, bronchitis, asthma, genito-urinary tract, arthritis rheumatism, chilblains, and are anti-carcinogenic

ORANGES

An orange taken with a meal helps iron absorption by two and a half times. It contains lots of vitamin C, folic acid and other minerals and is good for lowering cholesterol and combating infectious colds and 'flu. Also good for the circulatory system, and mildly laxative

PUMPKIN SEEDS

A nutritious snack food containing protein, zinc and iron as well as vitamins A and B

PEPPERS

Red and yellow peppers contain four times as much vitamin C as oranges!

POTATOES

The potato is one of our most valuable and nutritious foods – but eat them either baked or steamed, not fried! They are high in fibre and contain vitamins B and C

QUINOA

Grown in the Andes for over 5000 years, this seed/cereal has unique sustaining properties and significantly more protein than any other grain. It is rich in vitamins and minerals, has four times more calcium and more iron than wheat. This perfect food provides all the essential fatty acids

SHIITAKE MUSHROOMS

Immune-enhancing as well as having anti-carcinogenic properties, shiitake mushrooms are one of the very few sources of vitamin D, and also contain calcium and phosphorus. They induce the production of interferon, the body's own anti-viral chemical, and may have a potential to act against AIDS

also: almonds, bananas, celery, figs, grapes, lemons, molasses, oats, pulses, rice, sesame seeds, spinach, sprouted seeds, watercress, yogurt

Soya beans and products contain lecithin and folate and vitamin E. They help lower cholesterol and are helpful in heart and circulatory disease as well as protecting from some forms of cancer, containing isoflavones which decrease the risk of hormone-related cancers.

Vitamins and minerals

Busy women living at full stretch need to ensure that they get enough of all the right micronutrients, those vitamins and minerals which support body-health and protect the immune system, and also improve brain function. In a study at the University of New Mexico in the 1980s, researchers found the connection between good nutrition and cognitive performance to be closely linked. The B vitamins were linked to the ability for abstract thought, iron levels were associated with good memory and visual-spatial skills, and vitamins E, A, B6 and B12 were related to better recall.

Table of the most valuable vitamins

A

Sources: liver, oily fish, egg yolk, butter, cheese, carrots, squash, apricots, green leafy vegetables, raw pepper, sweet potato

Effects: antioxidant, helps circulation, healthy skin and immune system, protects brain cell membranes, night vision

B1 (THIAMIN)

Sources: cereals, sunflower seeds, pulses, peanuts, pork, liver, potatoes, nuts

Effects: production of energy, brain function, digestive function. strengthens heart muscle, prevents toxic build-up, use of protein

B2 (RIBOFLAVIN)

Sources: liver, wholemeal bread, milk, yogurt, eggs, meat, poultry, oily fish, fortified breakfast cereals

Effects: converts fat, sugar and protein to energy, repairs skin, regulates body acidity, needed for nails, hair and eyes, metabolic processes in brain, antidioxant

B3 (NIACIN)

Sources: Shreddies, tuna, lambs liver, peanut butter, mackerel, chicken, salmon

Effects: energy production, brain function, balances blood sugar, adjusts cholesterol levels, helps manufacture neurotransmitters, improves circulation

B5 (PANTOTHENIC ACID)

Sources: peanuts, raw mushrooms, eggs, walnuts, avocado, chocolate, pork, tomato puree

Effects: energy production, fat metabolism, healthy brain cells and nerves, skin, hair, anti-stress hormones

B6 (PYRIDOXINE)

Sources: Special K, peanuts, herrings, tomato puree, pork, avocado, poultry, fish, eggs, wholemeal bread, nuts, bananas

Effects: protein digestion, brain function, sex hormones, PMS, menopause, anti-depressant, diuretic, immune function, nervous system

B12 (CYANOCOBALAMIN)

Sources: yeast extract, liver, sardines, herrings, tuna, muesli, cheese, cod, lamb, dairy, seaweed, miso, alfalfa sprouts

Effects: helps carry blood oxygen, synthesis of DNA, use of protein, essential for energy and nerves, transports folate into cells, neuronal growth and vitality

BIOTIN

Sources: peanuts, hazelnuts, soya beans, Allbran, oatmeal, liver, oily fish

Effects: synthesis of fats,

healthy skin, hair and nerves, releases energy from food

FOLATE (FOLIC ACID)

Sources: yeast extract, green leafy vegetables, liver, broccoli, pulses, wheatgerm, breakfast cereals, bread, peanuts

Effects: relieves depression, growth of new cells, enhances cerebral circulation, nerves, energy

C

Sources: raw peppers, blackcurrants, citrus and berry fruits, strawberries, spring greens, sprouts, watercress, baked potatoes peas, leafy green vegetables, parsley

Effects: brain function, anti-oxidant, boosts immunity, builds up neurotransmitters, reduces cholesterol, strong bones, teeth and tissue, antiviral, antibacterial, detoxifies pollutants, prevents premature ageing of brain and nervous system

D

Sources: cod liver oil, herring, salmon, mackerel, sardines, eggs, margarines

Effects: needed to absorb calcium for strong healthy bones and teeth. Activated by sunlight

E

Sources: vegetable oils, sunflower seeds, nuts, avocado, butter, egg yolk, many vegetables, soya

Effects: anti-oxidant, skin, red blood formation, anti-ageing of brain and nervous system

K

Sources: most vegetables, especially green leafy ones

Effects: effective blood-clotter, forms proteins

Table of the most valuable minerals

CALCIUM

Sources: milk and dairy products, sardines, green leafy vegetables, sesame seeds, tahini, tofu, spinach, watercress

Effects: builds bones and teeth, good for the heart, nerves, muscle, skin

MAGNESIUM

Sources: wholegrain cereals, wheatgerm, pulses, nuts, sesame seeds, dried figs, green vegetables, bananas, soya products including tofu

Effects: bones and teeth, energy, carbohydrate metabolism, muscles, heart, nervous system

PHOSPHORUS

Sources: all plant and animal protein

Effects: healthy bones and teeth, releases energy in cells, absorption of many nutrients

SODIUM

Sources: table salt, yeast extracts

Effects: regulates fluid balance, essential for nerve and muscle function

ZINC

Sources: oysters, red meat, peanuts, sunflower seeds, cheese, dairy products, lentils, wholegrains, oats

Effects: growth, reproduction, immunity, learning and memory (helps over two hundred enzymes in the body and twenty in the brain)

IODINE

Sources: seaweed, seafood, green leafy vegetables

Effects: thyroid function, vitality, strong teeth, good circulation

IRON

Sources: bran flakes, sesame seeds, liver, liquorice, mussels, blackcurrants, sardines, dried figs, dark green leafy vegetables

Effects: deficiency causes anaemia

Natural supplements

Supplements and plant tonics improve and protect our natural good health which we need to look after while working at top level. A National Food Survey of 1993 found that the average person in the UK is deficient in eight out of thirteen vitamins and minerals, and a Government survey in the US found a deficiency of one out of ten. The supplements listed here all have a beneficial effect on brain function and some have a marked improvement in cognitive ability, as well as in physical energy. Once you start, be sure to take your supplements every day since irregular use doesn't work.

Taking a long look at your diet can help you assess whether you are getting sufficient vitamins and minerals for optimum health. Research trials have shown a direct link between higher IQ levels, better memory and concentration and a nutritious diet. Supplements make a difference.

Stress depletes us of essential nutrients, and food processing techniques and modern farming methods work against, not for us. Are you taking enough vitamin C? the B vitamins?

ALOE VERA

Nature's 'miracle plant' has been in use for over 2000 years. It is packed with nutrients including vitamins A, C and E, B vitamins, many minerals and twenty of the twenty two amino acids required by the body and proteins. Used for centuries for skin conditions, you can easily grow it as a houseplant: break off a leaf to treat a skin rash with the white sap. Aloe vera also acts on the inflammation of arthritis and rheumatism, and works as an anti-bacterial, antiviral and antifungal agent.

BACH FLOWER REMEDIES

'Treat the patient, not the disease' is the basic principle behind this system. It focuses on the patient healing herself by restoring balance in body, soul and mind. The flower essences are prepared from wild flowers and plants and administered in tiny doses.

ECHINACEA

North American Indians discovered that the plant *Echinacea purpurea* contains elements that maintain the body's resistance to disease, stimulating and supporting the immune system by activating white blood cells to fight infection, and triggering the production of natural killer cells and antibodies. Extracts of echinacea help boost your immune system to keep you in good health. Anti-fungal, antiviral and antibacterial, it has recently been used in AIDS therapy, and can be used to treat colds, sore throats, cystitis, tonsillitis, skin ulcers, herpes, eczema and psoriasis.

GINGKO BILOBA

Gingko enhances cerebral circulation, improving cognitive ability, poor memory and absent-mindedness. It helps migraines and headaches, stimulates the circulation preventing cold hands and feet.

HYPERICUM

The 'sunshine herb' hypericum provides a safe and effective alternative to synthetic antidepressants (it has been given the nickname 'Nature's Prozac'). It has no side effects, helps regulate sleep patterns and does not interact with alcohol.

This age old herbal remedy is out-selling Prozac – in Germany by a factor of ten to one. Its action benefits mood and emotional balance. It relieves mild to moderate depression, helps PMT, postnatal and menopausal blues, and Seasonal Adjustment Depression or SAD.

LECITHIN

Lecithin is important for optimum brain function since it improves cognitive ability and heightens mental agility by repairing and maintaining brain cells. It also metabolises fat and regulates cholesterol.

MAGNESIUM

Magnesium helps maintain the metabolic viability of brain cells and is a powerful free-radical scavenger. It helps increase the antioxidant power of vitamin E, deters blood clotting, thus decreasing the risk of heart attack.

SELENIUM

Selenium is a trace element found in wholegrains and vegetables and is nature's most effective mineral antidioxant, with a highly beneficial action on the brain. It is essential for healthy functioning of the immune system.

SPIRULINA

is a pond alga packed with iron, calcium, vitamin C, betacarotene, amino acids, fibre – and 60 per cent protein! It helps the body de-tox as well as being highly nutritious, and results in better energy levels and a sense of well-being.

Rescue remedy, a combination of five flower essences, is renowned for its calming and stablising effect in stressful situations.

Natural health & vitality

Natural good health

Boundless energy and good health are obvious requirements for busy women in the modern world, and a balanced way of life will go a long way to preserving vitality. But when you do fall ill, don't pop pills for a quick fix, instead think carefully about what you are putting into your body. Natural good health is a chemical-free zone, based as far as possible on natural plant remedies – and a positive attitude.

Basic good health is commonsense. Smoking, drugs and too much alcohol is bad for you, moderate exercise and a balanced diet are good for you. We have heard this so many times and yet we still ignore it, ultimately to our detriment. However, if you are fed up with your energy levels constantly flagging, or never quite shaking off that lingering winter cold, there are some simple steps you can take to improve the quality of your health dramatically – and have fun at the same time. When things do go wrong, as they are bound to, there are numerous age-old cures to be found in nature (see pages 151-154). There are so many ailments that can be treated or at least helped by everyday things around us, but we have become more and more disconnected from what grows in our environment or which is within easy reach in the kitchen cupboard and which can help us remedy common illnesses or traumas. There are natural supplements which can enhance the immune system and help commonplace disorders, saving us from spending a disproportionate amount of money on drugs. This is not to discredit the wonderful advances of modern medicine, but rather to complement them.

The body-mind connection

Natural good health implies emotional equilibrium – a healthy mind equals a healthy body. One of the single most influential factors on the immune system and the way we feel, is our attitude. With a positive attitude to life and its trials you have a better chance of good health, and are better able to cope with adversity. The way you think can determine your life span: optimists live longer than pessimists and have better general health. Research has shown that people with a negative outlook on life, gloomy, isolated, repressed individuals, are four times more likely to die within a few years of experiencing a heart problem, whereas optimists survive well beyond that time span. And optimists do better after surgery than pessimists: their natural killer cells rise by 13 per cent compared to a drop of 3 per cent among the pessimists.

The reason crying makes you feel better is that the chemicals built up during stress are released in tears. Research has shown that heart disease is caused as much by inhibited emotional expression – depression and suppressed anger for example – as by stress.

If you are not one of nature's optimists, you can train yourself by exercising your brain in cognitive thinking, learning to identify and change habitually negative thought patterns, including phobias, anger, anxiety and depression. Cognitive therapists (see *Useful addresses* page 204) work on the premise that it is your perception of events, and the way that you think about them, that cause your problems, not the events themselves.

The world's best selling drug is an ulcer treatment, handed out in shovelfuls to the stressed of the world in return for millions of dollars. This one example of the effect of stress on the body illustrates the intricate body-mind connection. Understanding the very physical impact that your state of mind can have on the body is foremost when looking to improve your health. Once we realise that many physical symptoms have a deeper, psychological source, we can begin to treat the whole, giving us the best chance of optimum health.

YOU ARE WHAT YOU THINK

The relatively new science of psychoneuro-immunology shows how mind and body are connected at the finest, most invisible levels. It has been shown indisputably that stress weakens the immune system and leads to illness. 'We can no longer consider the immune system in isolation from the rest of the body-mind-spirit and must seriously address the possibility that if diseases can be dramatically influenced by "state of mind", then perhaps altering a "state of mind" may be more beneficial than intervening solely at the level of the immune system,' writes Roger Booth, Senior Research Fellow at Auckland University School of Medicine.

THINK POSITIVE

Negative thoughts and emotions affect neuropeptides in the brain, which stimulate the endocrine system, flooding your body with hormones that depress the immune system, whereas positive thoughts and emotions encourage immune-enhancing hormones. So every time you succumb to anger, fear or anxiety you are delivering a shot of poison to the body. These toxic emotions double the risk of falling prey to disease.

That good emotional health can reduce the risk of physical illness is clearly shown in the incidence of back pain: one example of trials on nurses in Holland and Belgium shows that back pain was less likely to occur if their mental outlook on work was positive. In my experience, having been given a 'bad news' message by orthodox doctors, I maintained a positive attitude, believing (with the support of a brilliant physiotherapist) that there was an answer beyond passive acceptance ('it's wear and tear', 'it's your age'), painkillers or even surgery – and there was. Eighty per cent of us suffer from back pain at some time in our lives, and busy women are prime candidates with the stresses and strains – long hours sitting at a desk or lifting babies – that they are likely to encounter. But there is a natural way out of back pain, and you can do it yourself without recourse to drugs or surgical intervention (see pages 98-101).

EXPRESS YOURSELF

Sound emotional health presupposes the ability to express emotions freely and appropriately. Social isolation doubles the chances of sickness or death, whereas close emotional ties are good for your health: the help and solace of good companions cushion you from the impact of life's inevitable traumas.

Have fun to be healthy

Pleasure and relaxation are important components of good health: when people relax there is a significant increase in immune response. Enjoyable activities balance out the stresses of everyday life and there is medical evidence that happy people live longer. A sense of humour, the ability to laugh, to play, to have fun, to be silly (the word comes from a root meaning blessed, happy, joyful) all have their part in boosting the immune system.

HUMOUR IS THE KEY TO HEALTH

Laughter and relaxed happy states lower the blood pressure, raise the number and activity of natural killer cells, lower cortisol levels in the blood stream and increase the levels of immunoglobulin-A, an immunity antibody. This is merely proof of a very old idea: laughter is the best medicine. A South American rainforest community holds a festival of laughter and happiness whenever a member falls seriously ill, to speed healing and recovery. There is even an American Association for Therapeutic Humour. On top of that, laughing is good exercise: between one hundred and two hundred laughs a day (admittedly a lot) are equivalent to ten minutes hard rowing or jogging! Advice from the legendary Mae West: 'Just keep a spring in your heart and… ask yourself, "Where's my sense of humour?" If you can find one little piece of it, enough to make you smile, you'll take the heat off any situation and save wear and tear on your nervous system and digestion.'

Negative relationships take their toll, whereas positive ones, where you can unburden a troubled heart to a friend or supportive group, have been shown in research situations as well as commonplace experience to be immensely healing.

Keep smiling

When the psychologist Alfred Adler was working on auto-suggestion, he came to the conclusion that if you make yourself smile, you actually feel like smiling. Modern medical research shows that hormones are triggered from the brain which has simplistically taken the smile at its face value and by dint of association goes into the mode where it promotes feelings of well-being. So even if you don't feel like it, smile, and then you will feel like it! Happiness comes from attitude, it is not an external force. You can make your own without waiting for somebody else to supply it. There's no need for mood-altering drugs: you all have a useful chemistry laboratory up there inside the skull.

And from an immortally-youthful Hollywood star, Joan Collins:

TOP TEN TIPS

1. Think young and discard what doesn't work for you

2. Exercise often

3. Laugh a lot

4. Eat as much raw food as possible and only when you are hungry

5. Maintain your appearance

6. Drink one litre of water between meals

7. Stop smoking

8. Love someone or something, a lot

9. Have a glass of wine or a chocolate if you feel like it

10. Appreciate the beauty in the world around you

Your emotional health can be regarded as the most important part of your lifestyle check. How you feel about yourself and your life affects your physical health in powerful but insidious ways. Are you experiencing more than one of the following:

- **a lack of interest or enjoyment in life?**
- **a lack of drive or motivation?**
- **intense fatigue ?**
- **agitation and restlessness?**
- **poor concentration?**
- **not sleeping or too much sleeping?**
- **loss of sex drive?**
- **loss of self-confidence?**
- **feelings of vulnerability or fear?**
- **bursts of anger and impatience?**
- **feelings of being useless or inadequate?**

If so, you may need to change your diet (see Chapter 6), take more exercise (see Chapter 5), and look at changing quite a few other things in your life (your job, your partner, where you live, giving yourself enough me-time etc.) Stress is often an indicator of change, but only you can see what that change should be, and make it.

Whichever section of this book speaks to you, use it: have a new look at your home and see what improvements you can make to achieve a more harmonious lifestyle. Examine the impact of your work on your relationships and see whether the balance is right. Have you built in enough time for yourself, either to be alone or to relax with others? How good are you at managing your stress levels? Do you take enough of the right kind of exercise, and what is your diet really like? Are you looking after your health carefully enough, and do you give yourself enough soul time? Work on whichever areas need attention and meanwhile smile when you wake up in the morning, laugh, play and have fun,

Natural remedies

There are hundreds of age-old remedies for the minor ailments that beset us and our families all through our lives, which are based on the healing substances which nature provides for us. So instead of rushing off to the pharmacy, you can take responsibility for these common complaints. There are no side effects, they are inexpensive and they really work.

BURNS

Apply toothpaste for immediate relief, and the skin will not be marked

Apply the sap of aloe vera directly onto the skin

For severe sunburn, put 1-2 cups cider vinegar into the bath

COLDS, 'FLU, SORE THROAT

A brew which has stood the test of time: it stops the virus in its tracks taken at the outset of symptoms

Into 1.2 litres (2 pints) water put 1 teaspoon cloves, 1 cinnamon stick broken into small pieces, and 2.5 cm (1 in) root ginger, grated. Bring to the boil turn down the heat and simmer for five minutes. Remove from the heat, cover and leave to infuse for thirty minutes. Reheat gently, and strain into a mug. Add honey and lemon juice to taste, and finish with a sprinkling of cayenne pepper. Drink a cupful three times a day

Try a Chinese pressure point: press hard on the sole of the foot under the fleshy part of the metatarsal that leads to the middle toe

A mustard foot-bath is a classic remedy

Put 2 tablespoons mustard powder in a bowl of hot water, and sit with your feet immersed for twenty minutes. Then take yourself off to a warm bed and sweat out the infection

NATURAL TRAVEL TIPS FOR JETSETTERS *Drink lots of water during the flight, and choose an aisle seat so that you can get up to stretch your legs whenever you feel like it. Eat carbohydrates while flying (pasta is perfect) they produce natural melatonins which reduce jet-lag.*

COLD SORES

Dab with undiluted lemon juice (ouch!) or strongly caffeinated black coffee

Apply an alcohol-based aftershave, or vinegar, or TCP, to dehydrate the site

CONSTIPATION

Eat figs: very effective on an empty stomach first thing in the morning

Press the acupressure point on the bony V in the web between thumb and index finger. Repeat as often as needed

Eat lots of watermelon throughout the day: it cleanses the gut of waste material (see *De-tox* page 160)

COUGHS

Acupressure point: gently press the middle of the tongue with a tablespoon for three to four minutes

Drink lime blossom tea – it is sedative and calming. Blackcurrant tea soothes the throat. Thyme tea fights infection

Raise the head end of the bed on to bricks to stop coughing at night

CUTS

Sugar has a healing action and prevents scar tissue forming. Apply a little sugar to the cleaned cut and cover with gauze

Lemon or lime juice stops the bleeding, but it stings!

Crushed garlic dried into a powder was used on wounds by the Russian army in the First World War

CYSTITIS AND OTHER VAGINAL INFECTIONS

Drink a glass of water with 1½ teaspoons soda bicarbonate to neutralise the acidity of the urine, which is what causes the burning sensation

Eat live yogurt or take acidophilus supplements to restore the healthy balance of bacteria in the body

Drink a mixture of sage and peppermint tea

Cider vinegar is most beneficial added to a bath or taken internally with honey, 1 tablespoon in 200ml (8fl oz) water several times a day

DEPRESSION

You can help lift depression with certain 'mood-foods' such as grapes, wheatgerm, brewers' yeast, oats, buckwheat, molasses, berries, fish, seeds and nuts, shellfish, ginger, basil and rosemary

Hypericum (see page 142) tea: pour 1 cup of boiling water over 25g (1oz) of the herb. Steep for five to ten minutes, then strain and drink. You can do the same with lime blossom and rosemary

Add sea salt to the bath: 1-2 cups lifts the spirits. And sprinkle some on to your flannel for a skin scrub to promote a feeling of well-being

Add drops of bergamot and jasmine oil into a hot bath (8-10 drops of each) and soak for twenty minutes. Bergamot is uplifting and jasmine increases self-confidence

HEADACHE

Cut a fresh piece of root ginger and squeeze out the juice. Dab on to the temples

Bind wet mint leaves in a cloth and lay it across the forehead

Chinese pressure points: pinch the skin between the eyebrows with your index finger and thumb. Then pinch the skin in the midline of the back of the neck

HEARTBURN

Eat fresh pineapple after a meal. It has to be fresh – the canned fruit doesn't have the same effect. This is especially useful during pregnancy

Sleep on an incline, putting bricks under the head end of the bed

Simmer some bruised cloves in water for 10 minutes. Strain, dilute by half, and drink or massage clove oil over the stomach

IRRITABLE BOWEL SYNDROME

Avoid certain foods: you will find out which ones trigger your pain. Most commonly, high fibre, spicy or acidic foods

Massage the abdomen, or put a hot water bottle there

Do yoga (see pages 108-115). I had a yoga student who was completely cured of IBS by a regular practise of yoga stretches

INSOMNIA

Supplements of niacin (B3) have a sedative effect, taken only as directed

The Japanese recommend massaging the soles of the feet before retiring

Eat lettuce for supper – lactucarum, its white sap, is highly soporific

NIGHT CRAMPS

Put a cork at the end of the bed under the sheet – many people swear by this and it works for me

Drink tonic water before retiring – it contains quinine which seems to do the trick although nobody knows why

Keep the legs flexed by placing a pillow under the knees or against the feet

SORE THROATS

Usually a sign that a cold, cough or 'flu is on the way (see page 151)

Wring out a large handkerchief in cold water, lay it around the neck and tie in place with a woollen scarf on retiring to bed. An old, infallible country cure

Cider vinegar gargle: put 2 teaspoons cider vinegar, 1 drop lemon oil, 1 teaspoon honey into a cup and fill up with warm water. stir well and drink two to three times per day

STINGS

Make a paste of water and soda bicarbonate: it soothes the inflamed area and relieves pain

Put a drop of tea-tree oil on to a sting. Likewise lavender. You can put the oil neat on to a cotton bud

TOOTHACHE

Chew juniper berries to relieve the pain

Comfrey teabags, or ointment, applied to the painful gum reduces the swelling

Rub a cut lemon on to the affected tooth or gum

Alternative therapies

A research project at Sheffield University has shown that while public confidence in orthodox medicine has dropped to 40 per cent, it has risen by 40 per cent in alternative and complementary treatments. So if the scope of natural home remedies doesn't extend to more long-term or serious ailments, there are a number of other – increasingly tried and tested – routes to try. It is best to find a practitioner on recommendation rather than just searching the yellow pages, to make sure that you get the quality of care that you need. You may like to investigate pilates, tai chi, chi gong, light therapy, tuina, Ayurveda or any of the following.

Always check that an alternative practitioner carries a professional qualification and is registered with an organisation. They will be obliged to follow codes of conduct, and be more likely to come up to the standards of practice you would expect of anybody in private practice.

ACUPUNCTURE

Energy meridians of the body are unblocked and balanced by the insertion of fine needles into specific parts of the body, to regulate energy flow and restore health

ALEXANDER TECHNIQUE

Redirects the body to natural patterns and re-educates it to improve overall mental and physical well-being

AROMATHERAPY

Essential oils of plants are used to improve health and prevent disease

BACH FLOWER REMEDIES

The extracts of wild plants are used to restore emotional and psychological balance, heal trauma, and promote a positive outlook and good health

CHIROPRACTIC

Gentle manipulation corrects musculo-skeletal disorders, treating joints and muscles, and their effect on the nervous system (headaches, asthma)

CRANIOSACRAL

The use of gentle touch and subtle manipulations restores the even flow of cranial fluid through the body, healing and balancing body and mind

HEALING

The healer channels energy to the patient by touch, or even thought as in absent healing, to restore health and balance

HERBALISM

The use of herbs in healing, a practice based on centuries of use

HOMOEOPATHY

A treatment which works on the principle of 'like cures like', administering minute but potent doses of plant, animal and mineral substances

HYPNOTHERAPY

Creates a bridge from the unconscious to the conscious mind and facilitates changes when people get stuck with hidden behaviour patterns

IRIDOLOGY

A diagnostic method based on the appearance of the eye, where the nervous system comes to the surface of the body. Examination of the iris pinpoints weaknesses in the body

KINESIOLOGY

Certain muscle groups, related to specific body parts, are tested to detect imbalance or blockage. Light massage and dietary advice are given

NATUROPATHY

A largely preventative therapy concerned with emotional and physical balance. Diet, osteopathy and hydrotherapy also help the body recover from illness and rebalance itself

NUTRITIONAL THERAPY

Individual diet and supplement programmes enhance food assimilation, correct deficiencies, combat allergies and reduce toxicity

OSTEOPATHY

Working on the physical and mechanical framework of the body, manipulation and stretching techniques realign and release the body from pain

REIKI

A non-invasive method of spiritual healing where universal energy is channelled to the patient to encourage the body to heal itself

REFLEXOLOGY

The reflex points on the feet, corresponding to every part of the body, are worked on to unblock energy blockages and helping the body to heal itself

SHIATSU

Ancient Japanese 'finger-pressure' working on meridian points to balance the energy flow

Alternative treatments for irregular or painful periods, and the menopause: medical herbalism, homoeopathy and acupuncture all have a recognised therapeutic effect on female problems. Consult your local practitioner on good recommendation, or see* Useful Addresses *(page 204).

A quick lifestyle health check

We get into habits, some of them bad habits. It's easy to stop noticing them. From time to time it's a good idea to take stock and take a long and careful look at how healthy we really are as opposed to how healthy we think we are.

Diet, exercise and rest in the right proportions make a good solid combination for anyone who wants to look young and beautiful and stay that way.
Mae West, *My Autobiography*

FOOD
Daily calorie intake: women need 1500–2000, depending on how active you are.

At least 50 per cent of your daily intake should be carbohydrate, and less than 30 per cent fat.

You should eat around 450g (1lb) fresh fruit and vegetables every day – equivalent to five small helpings.

♦ **Eating little and often ensures a regular supply of healthy energy. Snack on fruit, fresh or dried, when you are hungry**

ALCOHOL
A drink at the end of the day can be a gentle relaxant, although it is by no means mandatory. There is evidence that small quantities of alcohol are beneficial to health, but too much can cause more than a headache: excess alcohol drains the body of essential nutrients, it highlights emotional instability, causes stomach problems and irritable bowel syndrome, high blood pressure and some cancers. It clouds the mind, affecting brain-power and spatial awareness.

♦ **Have one or two alcohol-free days per week. Take a weekend to de-tox (see pages 163-164)**

SMOKING
There is no safety advice here: smoking is dangerous to your (and others') health. A non-smoker living with a smoker runs a 23 per cent higher risk of heart disease than if they lived with a non-smoker. There are no safe limits. Between one and fourteen cigarettes a day increases by eight times your risk of dying of lung cancer. The only advice is to give it up. Now. Today.

♦ **Make your home a smoke-free zone (and insist that smokers do their business outside in the garden or street; give them an ashtray otherwise you'll find stubs in the flowerbeds or the driveway)**

FITNESS

How do you fare in these three criteria: stamina, strength, suppleness?

STAMINA

Measure your resting heart rate: before you get out of bed in the morning take your pulse. Press your fingertips against the artery at your wrist by the base of the thumb, and count the number of beats over a fifteen second period. Multiply by four: if your heart rate is under sixty – you are very fit; sixty to seventy – good; seventy to eighty – fair; eighty upward – poor (you may need to see a doctor)

♦ Make regular, gentle exercise a part of your day

STRENGTH AND SUPPLENESS

These are hard to measure, but *you* know! The best ways to improve both at the same time are yoga (see pages 108-115), dancing, gymnastics, swimming and the martial arts such as Tai Chi, Aikido etc.

♦ Do six complete rounds of Salute to the Sun (see pages 114-115) every day

WEIGHT

You all know what your 'right' weight is, by the way you feel energetically and emotionally. There are charts for so-called correct weight at stages of life, which are useful guides, but in the last analysis you are the best judge – if you are really honest with yourself! – of whether you are over or under weight.

♦ If you want to shed unwanted weight, follow the R.E.A.L. diet and food combining (see pages 129-132), and give yourself a cleansing weekend or fast de-tox (see pages 160-164). Go for regular long, brisk walks

HAIR

Thinning hair is often a sign of stress. Dry hair can be due to a deficiency of vitamins A, B12 or C, or iron and zinc. Dull hair may indicate stress and a poor diet, so have a look at ways in which you can improve them both, and add egg yolk to your conditioner after shampooing.

♦ Use a natural conditioner with no added chemicals on your hair (see pages 182-184), and check your diet

NAILS

Brittle nails cold be due to lack of iron or zinc. Ridges could be due to selenium deficiency (see page 143). Little white spots are less likely to be calcium deficiency than caused by bumps and bangs. Healthy nails are strong and pink: pale nails are a sure sign of nutrient deficiency or stress.

♦ Take mineral supplements to improve weak nails, and rub them with almond oil daily

TONGUE

Traditional Chinese medicine regards the state of the tongue as an indicator of health. Inflammation or soreness could be anaemia or vitamin B deficiency. Thick grey or white patches on the tongue are usually due to an accumulation of unwanted waste and a build up of toxins.

♦ Gently scrape the surface of your tongue with the tip of a spoon, then lightly brush it from the back to the tip. Do this every morning when you brush your teeth so that it becomes a daily habit. And drink more water: it cleans the system and prevents a build-up of bacteria

De-tox

All of these short regimes flush out the system and clean it of accumulated toxins, making you feel fresh and energetic. During the de-tox do not drink tea, coffee or alcohol. If two days on the fruit-only regimes is too tough for you, do just one, or allow yourself only a light (organic) salad in the early evening.

While you are on a two-day de-tox, build a programme of yoga stretches (see pages 108-115) and breathing (see pages 116-119) into your schedule. They will help you to strengthen the resolve that needs bolstering when thinking about the food you are not eating becomes distracting.

THE WATERMELON FLUSH

Take one to three days of eating nothing but watermelon (organic, if possible,) when they are in season – plentiful, blood-red and ripe. Eat as much as you like – including the seeds which are a source of fibre – and drink lots of water. You can add organic fruit juices if you like. This fruit fast gives the body a cleanse and a boost – although you may have headaches and other symptoms as the body releases its toxins. Once the body is cleansed you will feel wonderfully light and free and full of energy.

THE GRAPE FAST

Eat as many grapes as you like – well washed, since grapes are intensively sprayed during cultivation. Or (preferably), choose organic. Drink lots of mineral water and organic grape juice. Add herb teas if you wish. Practise this mono-fast for two days, then slowly come back to eating normally.

TWO–DAY MONTHLY DE-TOX

Reserve two days of every month to simply eat lots of steamed vegetables and salads, and drink only mineral water and herb teas. Start the day with organic fruit juice. If you practise this for two days every month the body regulates itself more healthily for the rest of the time. You will find yourself less likely to overeat, and you will gradually adjust to wanting more healthy foods, and less fatty and sugary ones.

In 1926 a South African natural healer called Johanna Brandt claimed to have cured herself of cancer by eating nothing but fresh grapes for weeks on end. A grape mono-fast has been shown to help numerous ailments including skin problems, and is an excellent way of shedding unwanted weight.

A weekend cleanse

The idea behind a weekend cleanse is to rest, re-balance, de-tox and enjoy yourself. For many busy women, it may seem impossible to put aside a whole weekend but it is truly worth it. It requires some thinking ahead to organise your space and to stock up with the things you will need so that you can relax into it when the time comes. Mark the weekend in your diary well in advance, otherwise it will never happen. You can give yourself one of the most positive holidays your body has had, all in the comfort of your own home. This space is caffeine and alcohol-free, to give the body a real chance to rest and clear itself. Just drink lots of water and herb teas.

A weekend alone to charge your batteries can seriously change your life for the better, giving you time to pamper your body as well as your soul – and in a guilt-free zone.

MAKE SPACE

When I do this I tend to choose a weekend when I have the house to myself: that is the ultimate luxury because you can do things in your own time, to suit you, without having to accommodate other peoples' needs. If this is not possible, discuss your needs with the people or person you live with and carve out a negotiated space for yourself. You have a right to a day or two to indulge yourself.

Tidy up the house in advance: throw out all the past sell-by-date food, old magazines and newspapers so that the atmosphere is clean and uncluttered. Throw out biscuits and savoury snacks and replace with fresh fruit.

BEAUTY TREATMENTS

A massage, pedicure, facial, manicure or even a haircut does wonders for the soul as well as the body so book a beauty treatment, at home if possible. Alternatively, if your budget does not stretch that far, set up your own DIY beauty treatments (see Chapter 9).

ORGANIZE THE LUXURIES

Select some of your favourite music to play, and get some books lined up that you have always wanted to read but haven't had the time. Change the bed linen and bath towels, and put a few drops of lavender oil on to the pillowcases.

STOCK UP IN ADVANCE

Shop for organic food, plus the drinks and herb teas you will need for the entire weekend, so that you can then sit back and relax and not have to think about shopping over the weekend. Buy some fresh flowers or new indoor plants. Buy in the ingredients you need for your beauty treatments, if you are doing them yourself, or some new natural products for your skin and hair.

SWITCH OFF THE PHONE

Outside pressures can easily sabotage the valuable space you are creating for yourself. So turn off the ringer on the phone, switch off the mobile, and give yourself a miniature holiday.

Two days of bliss

Go to bed early on Friday night after a light meal and herb tea (no alcohol.) On waking in the morning, lie quietly and breathe deeply. Breathe in, breathe out, following the mindful breathing (see page 200). Smile. Luxuriate in the warmth of the bed and enjoy the prospect of doing what you want for forty-eight hours.

A couple of days of pure personal space is hugely restorative. The rebalancing that it achieves has long-lasting effects, and you will remember this 'holiday' for a long time to come. Spoil yourself!

Take your time to rise, doing nothing in a hurry. Exfoliate the skin with a loofah or scrub-mitt. Spend at least half an hour in a relaxing aromatic bath (see page 169). Use your favourite essential oils – geranium is a truly lovely fragrance to start the day, so are lemon and ylang ylang.

After breakfast (see page 131) spend the morning reading, pottering, listening to music. Pick up a forgotten passion like painting, drawing or a craft. Daydream. Enjoy preparing your food, pick some flowers for the house, and don't feel that you should do anything! Spoil yourself, and enjoy the silence.

For lunch, either follow one of the de-tox ideas (see page 160), or make a delicious mixed salad. During the day drink lots of water – see if you can get through two litres. It flushes and cleanses the system and you will feel wonderful after two days of this. If you habitually drink lots of tea or coffee you may feel slightly headachy while the body adjusts to being caffeine-free. Pressing the acupressure point between thumb and forefinger for up to a minute can alleviate this.

In the afternoon, take exercise: take a brisk walk, go for a jog, go riding, cycling or swimming. Then snooze, read, listen to more music and give yourself a beauty treatment, for example, the facials (see page 176), followed by the foot soak (see page 189). Go to a quiet room to do some stretching or yoga (see pages 108-115). Keep yourself warm and comfortable at all times.

In the evening enjoy preparing a meal of your favourite food, or selecting from the ideas on page 131. If you are on the de-tox programme, lay the table beautifully even though you are not going to eat much! Think about the presentation, whether you are eating indoors or out if it is summer. Light a candle, play some music and eat slowly with relish and enjoyment.

I never watch television on these weekends, but I love to watch a film I have chosen specially to suit my mood or needs at the time. Late evening is a great time for meditation, so take as much time as you wish to sit quietly (see page 200). Then it is time to wash and prepare for sleep, with a relatively early bedtime.

Spend each of the two days following this kind of pattern, and you will feel both physically and mentally refreshed. Finally, write down some good resolutions to balance your life: eating-wise, exercise, health and relationships, and keep them handy afterwards.

Pure & simple beauty care

TRUE BEAUTY

You don't have to have model looks to be beautiful. Natural is beautiful. Energy is beautiful. A sense of humour and serenity are beautiful, and nothing is lovelier than a genuine smile. Radiant good health and the sense of being at ease in our bodies are more attractive than any make-up or the most expensive designer clothes.

Bliss in the bathroom

The bathroom is a place of supreme importance for busy women, a space to de-stress, to wind down, to be alone in the luxury of warmth and aromas, to take your time undisturbed and to enjoy solitude, with all the reviving, refreshing and healing effects of water treatments. Create your own personal spa in the sanctuary of your bathroom. And remember – this bastion of privacy is a guilt-free zone (the best ideas often come in the bath anyway…)

However humble your bathroom, it can still be turned into the ultimate pampering place. Decorate it with paints and tiles in any combination of blues and violets. These are the most restful, relaxing colours and there is an enticing spectrum to choose from: sky blue, cobalt, turquoise, ultramarine… If your budget is tight, bring in shades of blue with a hued shower curtain or plush towels. The room becomes an oasis, a retreat from the pressures of the world where you can drift and defuse tension in the blueness, and indulge in the scented comforts of a warm bath.

Stock the cupboard with some good-quality essential oils and get yourself a huge, soft, deep-pile bath-towel (this makes a great present). Hang it over the radiator while you bathe – or if you have a tumble-dryer, give it a whirl so that you climb out of the bath into an enveloping cloud of softness. If you like music to relax with, have a portable stereo in the bathroom and play your favourite music according to your mood. Hang a *do not disturb* notice on the door-handle, put the answering machine on, and your sanctuary is complete.

Aromatic baths

Use the best quality essential oils to make your bath both aromatic and therapeutic. Just add five to ten drops of oils that complement each other (three at most) to the bath and let them float on the surface of the water for a few minutes before getting in, to release their scent. Or mix the oils with a tablespoon of base oil before pouring it into the water, and it will absorb more easily into the skin. Light a candle and turn off the lights. Soak in the water for at least fifteen minutes, inhaling and enjoying the aromas. Don't leave the bathroom until you are truly ready.

Aromatic showers

2 tablespoons base oil (see page 174)

6-8 drops favourite essential oil

Mix together in a shallow bowl. Shower and wash all over. Then dip a damp flannel or sponge into the oil and rub all over the body until absorbed. Pat the skin dry. You can also sprinkle a few drops of your chosen oil into the shower-tray and when the water hits it it will release its aroma for you to inhale as you shower.

Natural beauty is about being yourself. This natural quality of beauty is for women who know that what matters is to feel beautiful. In the words of Naomi Wolf, 'The woman wins who calls herself beautiful and challenges the world to truly see her' **The Beauty Myth**

The way you treat your body (diet, exercise, health) and the way you think about yourself (positive self-regard) are reflected in your face and body language in ways that no disguise can hide.

SIMPLE BODY RUBS

Rub a handful of sea salt over your damp skin after showering, then shower off. If you mix the salt with olive oil or almond oil first, you get the double effect of moisturising and exfoliating. Bliss.

Mix 3 tablespoons of sweet almond oil with 3 tablespoons of fine oatmeal and mix to a paste with plain yogurt. Rub into any roughened skin, especially around upper arms and elbows.

Simple therapeutic baths

MILK AND ELDERFLOWER BATH

This wonderful bath softens and soothes the skin which feels beautiful afterwards. Just adding 300ml (½pint) milk to the water moisturises and nourishes the skin, an excellent solution if you live in a hard-water area.

2 tablespoons dried elderflowers (or 6 fresh flowerheads)

1 litre (1¾ pints) boiling water

6 tablespoons dried milk powder

Put the elderflowers into a large jug and pour the boiling water over them. Cover, leave to cool, then strain off. Mix the dried milk powder into the infusion and stir until dissolved. Add the mixture to a warm bath and soak for twenty minutes.

OATMEAL

Relaxing and soothing, this gorgeously soft soak rejuvenates the skin. Wrap 3 tablespoons medium oatmeal in a square of muslin (or the foot of old tights), tie up tightly with string and hang under the hot tap as you run the bath so that the water flows through it.

CIDER VINEGAR

Add 150ml (¼pint) cider vinegar to the bath water to soften and soothe the skin. Great for easing sunburn, too.

SALT

Mixing about 4 tablespoons of table salt to your bath heals and soothes the skin. Epsom Salts ease aching limbs and draw toxins from the body. Dissolve about 225g (8oz) in 1 litre (1¾pints) boiling water, add to the bath and soak for at least ten minutes before you start to use soap, which stops them from working.

SIMPLE MUD BATHS

Stimulating and cleansing, sloughing off dead cells, this amazing mud bath makes the skin tingle and feel really alive. Fill the bath with warm-to-hot water, and mix in 500g (1lb) Fuller's Earth (see *Useful Addresses* page 204). Add your favourite essential oil, and soak for fifteen minutes. Be careful as you step into the bath since it is quite slippery. No washing required (except for the bath which needs an extra clean but it's worth it.)

Use green clay (expensive) for acne and for wrinkles; or kaolin, a fine white clay (much cheaper), which improves the circulation and lymphatic flow.

Looking after your skin

If you analyse the basic ingredients of commercial cosmetics they amount to water, oil, wax, lanolin, alcohols and glycerine, so with very little trouble you can make your own. You can care for your skin (and indeed your hair, hands and feet) without depending on expensive products that sometimes contain allergenic substances and can create more problems than they solve. Select the purest of ingredients, and scent them with those natural essential oils best suited to your skin. Pamper yourself and feel good – without depleting the bank balance! Remember that your skin type may vary in that it may be drier in winter or summer, oilier around period time, and can change several times between puberty and menopause.

GOOD FOR THE SKIN

◆ **Fresh air, drinking lots of water, fresh organic food, sleep, relaxation and meditation, deep breathing, exercise, cleanliness**

BAD FOR THE SKIN

◆ **Exposure to sun, sun-beds, dry cold weather, air-conditioning, central heating, over-processed foods, excess caffeine or alcohol, stress, too much make-up, soap on the face, the effects of age, computer screens, and smoking**

Keep make-up to a subtle minimum. If you have a skin problem you wish to hide, it's better to cure it from the inside with a good diet, exercise and natural health remedies than to cake it with foundation and clog the pores.

Cleansing

Avoid using soap to clean the face as it is a detergent and dries skin out. Instead use a gentle oil, such as baby oil or a base oil, to remove make-up, or unperfumed cleanser to suit your skin type. Wipe off using soft tissues, making circles towards the centre of the face. Always make sure that your face is thoroughly cleansed at the end of the day so that the skin can breathe well during sleep.

Toning

Gentle natural astringents cleanse the skin and leave it refreshed. To make an infusion: use half a cup of chamomile, nettle or rose-hip tea (made with tea-bags, then cooled), and add two drops of the appropriate essential oil (see page 174). Apply gently with cotton wool.

TONER FOR OILY SKIN

A wonderful toning lotion which clears the skin and leaves it feeling soft.
Mix together 4 tablespoons each lemon juice, witch-hazel and rose water. Stir in 3-5 drops of lavender oil and pour into a clean bottle. Shake well, and store in a cool dark place for up to three months. Apply gently with cotton wool.

Moisturising

Simple plant oils nourish the skin naturally and restore its softness. Olive oil is one of nature's best and time-honoured moisturizers; or you can use sweet almond, wheatgerm or jojoba oils, preferably cold-pressed, as a base.
Mix 2 tablespoons of your chosen base oil, cold-pressed ones are the best quality (see *Useful Addresses* page 204), with 6 drops of a suitable moisturising essential oil.

ULTIMATE MOISTURISING CREAM

This is a fabulous cream – light but rich. I use it both morning and night, and its fragrance is exquisite. You can obtain an all-purpose cream base from suppliers of essential oils (see *Useful Addresses* page 204).

25g (1oz) cream or milk base

5ml peach kernel oil

5 drops ylang ylang

5 drops frankincense

5 drops neroli

Using a small wooden spatula, whisk the cream base with the peach kernel oil. Then gradually stir in the essential oils. Store in a jar in a cool, dark place (it keeps its perfume and texture for longer).

NOTE ON SENSITIVE SKINS

DON'T:
exfoliate, use alcohol-based products, expose skin to sun without sun-screen, use soap on the face.

DO:
de-stress, get more sleep, eat well.

Essential Oils for natural beauty care

Never use essential oils neat on the skin, and follow directions for use. Some oils should be avoided during pregnancy, so check carefully. Essential oils are powerful.

FOR THE BATH

Base oils: sweet almond, peach kernel, apricot kernel, wheat germ

Oils to relax with: basil, bergamot, cedarwood, chamomile, frankincense, hyssop, juniper, lavender, marjoram, melissa, neroli, patchouli, rose, sage, sandalwood, ylang ylang

Oils for balance: lavender, neroli, petitgrain

Oils to stimulate: cypress, eucalyptus, fennel, geranium, juniper, lavender, lemon, lemongrass, peppermint, pine, rosemary, thyme

Sensuous oils: neroli, orange, jasmine

Happiness oils: rose, sandalwood, jasmine, bergamot

FOR GENERAL SKIN CARE

Dry skin: chamomile, patchouli, rose, hyssop, sandalwood, geranium, lavender, ylang ylang

Oily skin: fennel, lemon, bergamot, cedarwood, lavender, geranium, juniper

Normal skin: chamomile, fennel, lavender, lemon, patchouli, rose sandalwood, geranium

Sensitive skin: neroli, rose, sandalwood, chamomile

FOR TONING

Dry or sensitive skin: rose, water or herbal infusion with rose oil or sandalwood

Oily skin: witch-hazel or herbal infusion with juniper or lemongrass

Normal skin: mixture of rose water and witch-hazel or herbal infusion with orange or lavender

FOR MOISTURISING

Dry skin: apricot (good for wrinkles), almond

Oily skin: coconut

Normal skin: wheatgerm (good for lines), avocado, peach

Sensitive skin: almond, peach (lots of vitamin A)

FOR FACIALS

Dry skin: benzoin, patchouli, frankincense, neroli (especially good around the eye area)

Oily skin: lavender

Normal skin: geranium, myrrh (especially good for ageing skin)

Sensitive skin: patchouli, neroli (for the eye area)

FOR STEAMS

To soothe: chamomile

To stimulate: lavender, peppermint, thyme

To heal: comfrey, fennel

To cleanse/de-tox: eucalyptus, juniper, rose, marjoram, rosemary, thyme

FOR HAIR

Dry hair:
Base oils: almond, jojoba,
Essential oils: rose, sandalwood, ylang ylang, lavender, geranium

Oily hair:
Essential oils: rosemary, basil, eucalyptus, cedarwood, chamomile, cypress, lemongrass, sage

Normal hair:
Essential oils: geranium, lavender, lemongrass, rosemary

FOR FEET

Soothing tired feet: spearmint

Relaxing and moisturising: lavender in jojoba or wheatgerm oil base

Stimulating and cleansing: eucalyptus, tea tree

Deodorising and soothing: cypress, lavender

Refreshing and calming: rosemary and lavender in almond oil

Stimulating circulation: rosemary

Natural beauty treatments for the face

The face deserves to be looked after. Its intricate muscles work hard, and the skin gets more exposure to sun, dirt and pollution than other parts of the body. Cleansing it, nourishing it and keeping it moist make up for the wear and tear of everyday life.

Steams and masks

SIMPLE STEAMS

The object of a facial steam is to release stale oils from the pores and loosen debris sticking to the skin. It feels delicious afterwards. Fill a medium size bowl with hot (not boiling) water. Add up to five drops of a cleansing oil (see page 174), drape a towel over your head and sit with your face about 45cm (18in) from the water, inside the tent of the towel. Breathe deeply for about five minutes, allowing the steam to permeate the pores, both moisturizing and cleansing your skin.

NATURAL CLAY MASKS

Natural clay masks have a detoxifying effect on the skin and work to best effect after steaming. They refresh and nourish your skin with minerals, restoring its balance and repairing its texture. The skin looks radiantly clear after a clay mask, and feels fresh and velvety. It costs next to nothing but is a great investment. Fuller's earth is a natural powdered clay which you mix to a paste with warm water. Add yogurt and/or oatmeal for texture. Or use 'fine green clay', available from specialist stockists (see page 205) which has a high mineral content and is naturally healing and absorbent. It is very good for oily skin

and can be used freely: it makes a toning and detoxifying face mask and stimulates the circulation. You can also use it as an internal cleanser (1 teaspoon in a glass of water).

To make a clay mask, mix about 1 tablespoon of clay with enough spring water to make a spreadable paste, mixing with a small wooden spatula. Add the required essential oils, and allow to soak for a few minutes. Then smooth on to the face with the spatula and allow to dry. Leave on for ten minutes if you have a dry skin, fifteen to twenty minutes if oily. Then wash off with lukewarm water, and splash the face with cold water, or wipe with rose-water. If you have very dry skin, try using egg yolk to mix the paste; if oily, use rose-water.

A SIMPLE COMPRESS

This quick fix moistens the skin and relaxes the face. Great for when time is running away with you.

Add 5-8 drops of your preferred essential oil (see chart) to 150ml (¼pint) warm water.

Soak a flannel in the solution, squeeze out any excess liquid and lie down in a quiet place with the flannel over your face, leaving the nostrils free. Remove after ten minutes.

ALTERNATIVE MASKS:

FOR OILY SKIN:
fine oatmeal mixed to a paste with witch-hazel.

FOR DRY SKIN:
honey, egg yolk and almond oil.

FOR DULL SKIN:
mashed peach or banana mixed with egg yolk.

OATMEAL FACE MASK

A wonderful exfoliant which leaves your skin feeling brilliant, and so soft. This mask can be quite messy, so wrap an old towel around your shoulders to protect your clothes, and lie down with a towel over the pillow to catch any escapes.

1 heaped tablespoon medium oatmeal

rose-water to mix to a paste

Spread on to the face, avoiding the eye area, and lie down for twenty minutes. Then remove over the sink by rubbing it with your fingertips – it peels off like eraser-rubbings. Then wash the skin gently with lukewarm water.

Facials

RICH AVOCADO FACIAL

You can 'feed your face' (literally) with oil-rich avocado and nutritious honey.

1 tablespoon ripe avocado, mashed

1 teaspoon honey

3 drops of cider vinegar

enough sesame oil to work to a spreading consistency

Apply the mask to the face carefully, avoiding the eye area. Lie down, with the eyes closed for fifteen to twenty minutes. Wash off with warm water, and finish with rose-water if desired.

FACIAL FOR TIRED SKIN

Rejuvenating natural ingredients leave the skin feeling smooth and refreshed.

2 tablespoons ripe avocado

1 teaspoon clear honey

1 teaspoon lemon juice

1 teaspoon plain yogurt

Mash together and leave to chill in the fridge for half an hour. Then apply to the face and lie down for ten minutes. Wipe with lukewarm water, and dry gently.

30 MINUTE FACIAL ROUTINE

5 mins:	**Apply olive oil with soft tissue**
2 mins:	**Wipe with rose-water**
5 mins:	**Apply avocado face mask**
15 mins:	**Lie down with slices of cucumber on eyes**
2 mins:	**Apply moisturising cream**
1 min:	**Final cleanse with rose-water**

Rose water has universal appeal, its scent evocative of the fragrances of summer. Applied with soft cotton wool, its action on the skin is softening and cleansing, and leaves you feeling fresh.

Eye power

Dark circles and puffiness around the eyes are caused principally by lack of sleep, or dehydration. When we feel dreadful, we look dreadful – especially around the eyes. Enough restful sleep (Chapter 9), and drinking enough water (see page 134) both go a long way to maximising the beauty and clarity of the eyes. Taking regular exercise makes a difference too. Excess alcohol or salt in the diet don't help, and cigarette smoke dries them out and wrinkles the delicate skin around the eyes.

SILK EYE PILLOW

Cut two pieces of soft cotton, silk or velvet 25cm by 10cm (10in by 4in). Leave a seam allowance of 1.5cm (½in) all around and sew up on three sides, leaving one short side open.

Stuff with 125g (4oz) rice, plus a few fresh or dried lavender buds if you can get hold of them: the scent of lavender is soothing and relaxing.

Turn in the edges of the short side and sew up neatly. Alternatively a mixture of 125g (4oz) flax seeds, lavender and mint is lovely.

Heavy, oily night creams may produce puffiness because they block the lymph nodes. Try aloe vera cream or gel on the fragile skin under the eyes: it improves the texture by stimulating the production of collagen and elastin, leaving the skin looking less wrinkled. A scientist testing its effects always put it on her left hand and the skin hardly aged!

For days, however, when the eyes are tired, the bags are heavy and the circles dark, try the following:

- **Rub a slice of raw potato gently into the skin under the eyes**
- **Rub ice cubes over the bags around the eyes**
- **Splash cold water on to your closed eyes about twenty times, then pat dry with a soft towel. This stimulates the blood flow and tones the eyes**
- **Lie down and cover the eyes with slices of cucumber for five to ten minutes**
- **Put used, cold wet teabags over the eyes for five to ten minutes**
- **Wrap ice cubes securely in cling-film and place over the eyes for five minutes**
- **Place cotton wool pads soaked with witch-hazel or Indian tea**

A FINGERTIP MASSAGE

Place a little sweet almond oil or Ultimate Moisturising Cream (see page 173) on to each ring finger and place each finger in the outer corner of each eye. Lightly stroke the fingers towards each other following the line of the socket.

Press down for a moment on the inner corner of each eye.

Then sweep the fingers up along the upper edge of the eye socket towards the temple, with a slightly firmer pressure along the eyebrow.

FOR SORE, TIRED OR PUFFY EYES

Pour boiling water to cover two chamomile teabags. Leave until cold, then chill in the refrigerator. Squeeze out excess water, lie down and place over the eyes. Relax for ten minutes.

FOR ITCHING OR SENSITIVE EYES

Eyebright is a natural anti-inflammatory herb, and is useful for eyestrain and all types of infections. Drop 30 drops of tincture of eyebright into a glass of rose-water (or use cool, boiled water). Soak cotton pads in this and bathe the eyes regularly morning and evening.

CORNFLOWER DECOCTION

For tired watery eyes and to reduce inflammation, this soothing remedy is a dream. Put 25g (1oz) fresh cornflowers into 500ml (1pint) and boil until reduced by half. Allow to cool completely before using then dab on gently with cotton wool.

Beauty from the kitchen

The ingredients for quite a few natural beauty treatments can be found in the kitchen cupboard. Nature's very best skin and hair conditioner, for example, resides in the olive oil bottle. It was used by the ancient Greeks, and possibly even before, as the foundation of beauty care. I keep a bottle on my bathroom shelf and use it regularly on my skin and hair.

Use egg yolks, honey, glycerine and avocado on dry and sensitive skins.

Use wet muslin for applying and wiping your oils and treatments – it lightly exfoliates the skin and can be washed and re-used

Over the centuries women have discovered that many other everyday foods have similar nourishing effects: avocado, yoghurt, milk, lemon, eggs and certain fruits for example. The obvious advantage of beauty products from the kitchen cupboard is that thay are to hand, they are cheap, and they have none of the side-effects that commercial products can have, particularly on sensitive skins.

◆ Dab small amounts of olive oil on to the skin with cotton wool pads to keep it soft and supple. It is nature's best moisturiser. Let it soak into your face while in a hot bath

◆ The lactic acid in yogurt cleanses and nourishes the skin. Likewise using milk or buttermilk as a toner gives it a natural first aid treatment

◆ Rub a little lemon juice into oily skin to tone and refresh. Great for scaly elbows, too

◆ Egg-whites dry and tighten the skin and are excellent for oily skins

◆ Rub a strawberry into oily patches of facial skin

◆ If you have a dry skin, home-made mayonnaise is your best natural moisturiser from the kitchen: it softens and enriches the skin

◆ For a great skin toner, rub the inside of watermelon, banana or papaya skin onto your face

◆ Use sesame oil for stretch marks

◆ Removing make-up with white vegetable fat also acts as a deep moisturiser

◆ Cucumber whizzed in the blender gives a juice that is a brilliant skin freshener

◆ Fine oatmeal is an exfoliant: mix it into your normal moisturiser and massage the skin gently

TOP TIPS

These are some easy-to-follow tips to keep you looking good all year round. Ice-cold water splashed on to the face gets the circulation going and brings natural colour to the face. Spray the face with a fine atomiser of spring water after cleansing but before moisturising and the cream will lock in the moisture. In cold weather you need to moisturise your skin more frequently, so use a little more cream, rubbing it in gently. Pierce a capsule of vitamin E oil and rub gently into the face – it is one of the best and simplest of moisturisers. Use Vaseline as lip-gloss: it keeps the lip skin beautifully soft. Keep your hands lovely with the Hand Exfoliant (see page 187).

Hair care the natural way

The best nutrients for your hair can be found in your everyday diet: lots of fresh fruit and vegetables, live yogurt, seaweed, pulses, wholegrains, almonds, millet, figs and dates, oily fish – and lots of water.

More than any other single element of our appearance, our hair defines us. It gives out more information about us than we subconsciously realise. The condition of your hair says much about your general health, and many hair problems are linked as much to diet as to emotional health. And there is power in hair: remember Samson and Delilah? On a good hair day you feel as though you can conquer the world. A bad hair day can, on the other hand, lower morale and confidence and detrimentally affect how you interact with others. So looking after your hair pays big dividends. As with skin beautiful hair works from the inside out. Oily hair can sometimes mean a vitamin D deficiency; dry or brittle hair indicates a lack of essential fats. Poor growth or dull colour may mean a zinc deficiency, and hair loss indicates bad general nutrition. If you eat well, exercise, get lots of fresh air and sleep well, your hair is likely to have shine and bounce to it. The No-Nos are excessive dairy, caffeine, cola, chocolate, sugar, salt and processed foods (so what's new?) And of course smoking. Don't over-expose hair to hot sun or central heating, and if you are stressed do what you must to de-stress (see Chapter 4). It will do wonders for both your skin and your hair.

Treat your hair as a precious commodity, give it natural oils to replenish and condition it, have a good haircut regularly, and use good quality brushes (not nylon) and combs. Brushing your hair thoroughly releases its oils, so don't stint; use minimal heat on your hair because it dries it out and makes it brittle. Avoid the use of chemicals as far as possible in hair products (use henna treatments for colour in preference to chemical dyes). Appreciating the natural state of your hair is the best thing you can do for it: don't try to straighten it if it is curly or curl it if it is straight. Go with nature and do as little as possible to interfere. Just give it as much conditioning and nourishment as it needs, to enhance its natural beauty.

OLIVE OIL CONDITIONER

Nature's very best conditioner is to be found in the kitchen cupboard: olive oil. So whether your hair be brittle, dry, damaged by chemicals (tinted, permed, streaked, over-exposed to sun) open the kitchen cupboard and go to work.

You can apply the oil warm or cold. Just pour a little into the cupped palm of your hand and palm it over your hair. Repeat until all the hair is lightly covered. Then brush the oil in thoroughly, wrap your hair in a scarf or towel specifically used for the purpose (just wash it each time) and leave to soak in for at least half an hour. I often leave it for longer.

When it comes to washing your hair just rinse out the oil first and then shampoo. This simple treatment leaves the hair with excellent shape and texture. A variation is the olive oil and egg conditioner:

1 egg

olive oil

a little chopped chilli pepper (optional)

Crack the egg into a bowl. Pour some olive oil into one half shell and mix in thoroughly. Add the optional chilli pepper, which stimulates the scalp. Dampen your hair and towel-dry. Massage the conditioner into the scalp and the ends of the hair, and cover with a shower cap for twenty minutes. Rinse out the mixture before shampooing as normal.

HOT OIL TREATMENTS

Choose a base oil for your hair type (see page 174), from jojoba, almond, sunflower, apricot kernel, avocado, evening primrose. (Olive oil has a very strong scent and will overpower the essential oils so is best used on its own.)

SCALP MASSAGE

Choose up to three essential oils to suit your hair type, and add 4-5 drops of each (12-15 in all) to 2 tablespoons base oil (unless you have very long hair in which case increase the quantity). Warm the blended oils in a bowl by standing it in simmering water. Massage into the scalp, wrap in a warm towel and leave for fifteen minutes before shampooing.

After shampooing, massage your scalp vigorously with strong movements of the fingertips (using your fingerpads rather

Shampoos are made up of water, perfume and detergent. The latter breaks down the natural oils in the hair, so use as little as possible at each wash.

Lemon juice highlights blonde hair, and diluted cider vinegar highlights brown or red hair. Cider vinegar is a great toner for both the skin and hair.

than your nails!) making circular movements over the head. Work from the forehead, frontal hairline, temples and sides over the crown of the head and down to the base of the neck. Spend about five minutes on this before applying your conditioner. Leave the conditioner to soak in for at least five minutes before the final rinses.

HAIR REVITALISING TREATMENT

This beautifully aromatic oil brings life and shine back to dull or damaged hair, and smells wonderful. I have used it for years and find that it makes all the difference to the body and texture of my very fine, rather dry hair.

30ml extra virgin olive oil

10ml jojoba oil

10ml wheatgerm oil

8 drops geranium

12 drops lavender

6 drops patchouli

Pour the vegetable oils into a clean 50ml bottle, add the essential oils and shake well. Apply the oil to dampened hair, rub in well and leave on for twenty minutes. Repeat the treatment every four to six weeks.

DANDRUFF

If you suffer from dandruff, massage a cup of fresh apple juice into the hair, working from the roots down to the tips. Then dilute 2 teaspoons of apple cider vinegar in a cup of water and use this as a rinse. You will begin to see a difference after the second or third application.

COMMONSENSE TIPS

- **Don't wring out your hair hard after washing – it is at its weakest when wet and this breaks it. Squeeze out excess water gently before wrapping it in a towel**
- **Don't over-use the hair-dryer. It makes hair dry and brittle. Let it dry naturally**
- **If your hair goes frizzy in dry conditions, rub a drop or two of baby oil into the palms of your hands, and smooth them over the hair. Brush out gently. Almond or avocado base oil also do the trick**
- **Don't use too much shampoo – it is a detergent and strips the natural oils from your hair. To counteract its alkaline content, put a tablespoon of lemon juice or cider vinegar into the final rinse**
- **Wash your hairbrush and comb in warm water with a little washing soda to get them really clean**
- **Rinsing hair in lukewarm mint tea helps oily hair**
- **A hair-pack of natural yogurt softens and purifies the hair**
- **Use a final cold rinse to make hair extra shiny**

FOR OILY HAIR

- **Check your diet, and don't spend too much time in centrally heated places**
- **Use plastic brushes rather than bristle, and massage your scalp to regulate the sebaceous glands that produce the oil**

FOR NORMAL HAIR

- **Occasional hot-oil treatments using any base oil you prefer keep it healthy and glossy**

Beautiful hands and nails

Add a little bath oil to the water when you wash your hands, to keep the skin and nails from drying out. It softens cuticles too.

I once heard someone say that the hands are the windows of the soul. It's an interesting thought: perhaps our hands do say more about us than we realise. They are expressive, they are sensitive, they work very hard. They deserve to be looked after: they have more brain cells attached to them (along with the mouth) than any other single part of the body. Our hands are also one part of the body which show early signs of ageing. They are almost always exposed to the sun so lather on that sunscreen! It really takes no time at all to look after your hands: keep a small tube of handcream in your bag so that you can apply it regularly – even travelling to work on the train or bus. Keep a nail file and clippers handy also – at your desk, in the kitchen, in your bag or in the car – to keep nails in shape or to file them as soon as they split or break.

Protect your hands whenever possible: wear cotton gloves for gardening, and lined rubber gloves for washing or washing up as water weakens and breaks nails (the lining protects the nails from becoming soft). Use a gentle soap with added oils, and moisturise immediately after washing, this also keeps the cuticle supple and prevents it from cracking.

Find a good handcream that suits your skin (as chemical-free as possible) and keep a tube in every room in the house, as well as in the office, so that you can moisturise your hands regularly.

If your hands get ingrained with dirt, after painting or gardening for instance, coat them with Vaseline, leave it to absorb for a minute or so and then wipe off with tissues rather than scrubbing them with soap (which dries them out).

Stress can also damage the strength and growth of your nails, so if this is the problem read the chapter on Surviving Stress (see page 65).

HEALTHY HANDS

- **If the hands become especially dry, rub a few drops of sweet almond oil or jojoba oil in and massage well**
- **After gardening clean your hands with a mix of about 1 tablespoon each fine rock salt and olive oil, to cleanse and moisturise at the same time**
- **If your nails are weak and brittle, make sure you are getting enough zinc, iron, calcium and selenium in your diet (see page 143). Fish oils and evening primrose oils are important for healthy nails**
- **Add a little bath oil to your hand-wash to nourish and moisturise the nails**
- **If you use nail polish, use an acetone-free nail remover (acetone dries them out and splits them). Rub the nails with almond oil afterwards**
- **Rub fragile and flaky nails with a base oil (apricot kernel, sweet almond, wheatgerm or jojoba) to strengthen them, especially after removing nail polish**
- **Mix equal quantities of castor oil and glycerine and use as cuticle softener**

NIGHT CARE SPECIAL

Soak your hands in warm water with a little bath oil added, then dry off and rub in lots of extra-rich cream. Put on surgical gloves and go to bed: you wake up with hands like silk (this is for people who live alone!)

RESTORING OIL MASSAGE

When hands get dry and tired, rub in several drops of this oil until well absorbed. Stretch the fingers as you work, massaging from the tips of the nails to the cuticles and up to each finger knuckle. Make deep stroking movements over the back and palm of the hand, then pull hard on each finger in turn to release tension.

1 teaspoon sweet almond oil

5 drops each patchouli, lemon, and lavender

NAIL OIL

For extra strong and shiny nails, this home-made concoction works a treat.

2 teaspoons walnut oil

2 drops each frankincense and myrrh

Mix well. Rub into nails daily.

SOFTENING HAND LOTION

Mix 50ml coconut milk with an equal amount of glycerine, and rub a little into the hands for five minutes. Massage well before rinsing. Store in a cool place for up to a week. To really pamper your hands, use a face mask (see page 175) on them once a week.

HAND EXFOLIANT

This sloughs off dead cells, and cleanses and moisturises all in one. A great little recipe from the kitchen cupboard which leaves the hands beautifully soft.

25g (1oz) ground almonds

1 teaspoon clear honey

2 teaspoons walnut or sunflower oil

1 teaspoon lemon juice

Mix together to a thick paste. Rub a heaped teaspoon all over the hands for two to three minutes and rinse off.

Fabulous feet

Massage your feet after bathing or showering, using one of the oils on page 174. Peppermint is wonderfully reviving if you need a new lease of energy.

Feet are important. We hide them away in shoes all their lives and neglect them. To our detriment. Feet work hard so we do well to afford them due reverence: we walk over 70,000 miles in an average lifetime. So why not look after them just as we look after our face or our hands? There is such refreshment in a foot soak or a pedicure, and you feel the effects of the treatment throughout the whole body (and mind). Make a regular date with yourself to look after your feet. Be kind to them!

They say that when your feet hurt you hurt all over – and the strain shows on your face. So if your feet are killing you, throw out those uncomfortable shoes, buy comfortable ones, and spend more time in bare or stockinged feet. Let your feet breathe.

Use moisturising creams and lotions on your feet – they get just as dried out as hands do. Massaging in a little cream before going to sleep gives you a more restful night. Aloe vera lotion is softening as well as healing, and helps to smooth any rough skin on the soles of the feet.

TREAT YOUR FEET

- **Give yourself regular foot-baths (see opposite). They are wonderfully revitalising and soothing**
- **Polish the rough skin on your feet with pumice – or a handful of wet sea salt**
- **Gently rub sweet almond oil into toenails and push back cuticles with a cotton bud, rather than using chemically-based cuticle remover**
- **If you suffer from chillblains, mix 1 tablespoon sweet almond oil with 3 drops of geranium oil and 1 each of lavender and rosemary. Rub in morning and night**

Foot baths

Soaking your feet in water, with oils added, is powerful pampering. It de-stresses and revitalises the whole body. I bought myself a mini foot-spa which has a whirlpool action and a knobbly floor for hitting the relevant pressure points: it is pure bliss.

You can just as well soak the feet in a plastic bowl, and place a selection of marbles in the bottom. Arm yourself with a large towel before you start, to wrap the feet in afterwards for five minutes to relax as they dry off. Indulge in the soak for at least fifteen minutes.

A SUPPLY OF OILS FOR FOOTBATHS

Put 50ml base oil (see page 174) into a small screw-top plastic bottle. Add 12-15 drops of essential oil (see page 174), and store in a cool place. For every footbath, add 2-3 capfuls of the scented oil.

FABULOUS FOOT CREAM

This is the ultimate in foot pampering.

50g (2oz) cream base

6 drops apricot kernel oil

6 drops frankincense

6 drops geranium

6 drops benzoin

Using a small wooden spatula, mix the base with the apricot kernel oil. Then whisk in the oils and mix well. Rub the cream into the feet, massaging them as you do so. Press between the toes, pulling the toes upwards to stretch them. Work the cream into dry or rough skin, and make sweeping movements up along the arch of the foot. Massage into the back of the heel up towards the ankle, and around the front too. Massage the soles of the feet thoroughly. Your feet feel wonderfully free after this work-over. This pedicure is an ideal treatment for the Two Days of Bliss (see page 164). Line up all the ingredients you need and treat yourself.

45 MINUTE PEDICURE

15 mins:	**Footbath – see above**
5 mins:	**Exfoliate with pumice or handful of wet salt**
10 mins:	**Apply Fabulous Foot Cream with massage**
5 mins:	**Massage almond oil into nails and push back cuticles**
10 mins:	**Trim nails and apply nail colour if desired**

Pamper yourself

When life becomes all too much, taking time out to pamper yourself is probably the best investment you can make in your energy. The occasional pedicure, manicure or facial, sauna or hydrotherapy treatment go a long way to recharging batteries when they are low. A regular reflexology session is great, too, releasing tension while also treating any problems that may be exacerbated by fatigue or stress. Allowing someone else to do something for you, to you, makes a pleasant change from the do-it-yourself mentality that busy women become used to. So remember Julia's Test (see page 58) and spoil yourself. Remember that you deserve it!

For the purposes of research for this book I took myself off to a Spa Day at a famous London hotel – and went to heaven. A jacuzzi and steam room were mine to linger in after a refreshing power-shower. An exfoliating body scrub followed, then I soaked in a hydrotherapy bath which contained marine algae and essential oils to detoxify and balance. Powerful jets shot arrows of water at specific points to tone and stimulate pressure points, and to enhance lymphatic drainage. I then had the full body massage of my life, followed by a light but elegant lunch sitting by a fountain wrapped up in a huge white towelling robe. I then lay down in the ionising room on a water-bed to snooze and digest, bathed in ultra-violet light, and my bliss was made complete with a wonderful deep-treatment facial. I floated out on to the busy London streets a new (albeit poorer) woman. That was completely over the top: you don't have to go for broke (although it's nice…) So go on, treat yourself!

Find the best health spa near you and make the choice from: sauna, steam room, power-shower, jacuzzi, aromatherapy massage, hydrotherapy bath, facials, mud treatments, body wrap, paraffin wax treatments, lymphatic drainage massage, body scrubs, water bed, manicure, pedicure, Thai massage, Swedish massage, reflexology, eye treatments, Cathiodermie treatments, craniosacral therapy.

Soul time

Soul time

Space, solace, solitude, silence, softness, stillness, simplicity, soul – from underneath an avalanche of sensory overload that threatens to smother us, we hear these words with a wave of relief (stop is the first…) Each represents an element of peace and inner calm. The great traditions of mysticism from many cultures have produced volumes of wisdom on these elements (see *Bookshelf* page 204), but we also need to define for ourselves our individual priorities in terms of soul needs.

A regular meditation practice makes for excellent soul time (see page 199) but the most important thing is to create a space which suits you.

Soul-time connects you with your fundamental reality – it puts your life into perspective – and you are most likely to connect with it when you are alone. Such soul moments give glimpses of a personal insight and it is astonishing how easily our lives are choked by the silting of daily actions, reactions and conditioning.

Personally and along with many others I find solace in nature walking in the early mornings as the earth starts to breathe, or smelling lavender at evening in a darkening garden, or looking at shadows in the water. The essence of this solace is space, the personal space just to be. Yet, however alone one may be, one is never lonely. Research into the physics of participation psychology has proved that merely looking affects electrons being looked at: they are seen under scanning to actually change. Interdependence becomes more than idea, it is an actual experience.

Some degree of solitude is necessary for inner balance, and it is nourishing to the psyche. You need to balance time alone with time spent with others to achieve self-knowledge and understanding. Human beings easily become alienated from their deepest needs and feelings. Learning, thinking, innovation and maintaining contact with one's own inner world are all facilitated by solitude.

THE VALUE OF SILENCE

Periods of silence are essential to vitality, especially for creative people. Deep inner silence precludes the necessity to verbalise, and creates space for the soul. Cultivation of inner silence has long been recognised in many cultures as a cornerstone of spiritual growth. There is a form of listening meditation where you simply concentrate your attention on any sounds there may or may not be. A distant car, a bird singing, a dog barking, a clock ticking, the wind in the trees, or rare moments of complete silence. When the mind begins to wander, just pick up these sounds again. There is no better way of quietening the tumult of the mind.

SIMPLICITY

Simplicity can be deeply refreshing. Less is more. So simplify your life. Clear out the clutter (see page 24), cultivate the doctrine of enough (whoever knows that enough is enough will always have enough; they will always be rich), and take a new look at your life in which you count the positive things that you have. Fundamentally we all know that there is more to life than getting and spending, that there is a wellspring of peace and happiness that comes only through the spiritual side of ourselves. But we ignore this intuition at some cost to ourselves because opening ourselves to the beauty and mystery of the soul enriches life immeasurably and puts into perspective that 'other' world of busy-ness, business, the journey in the world of things.

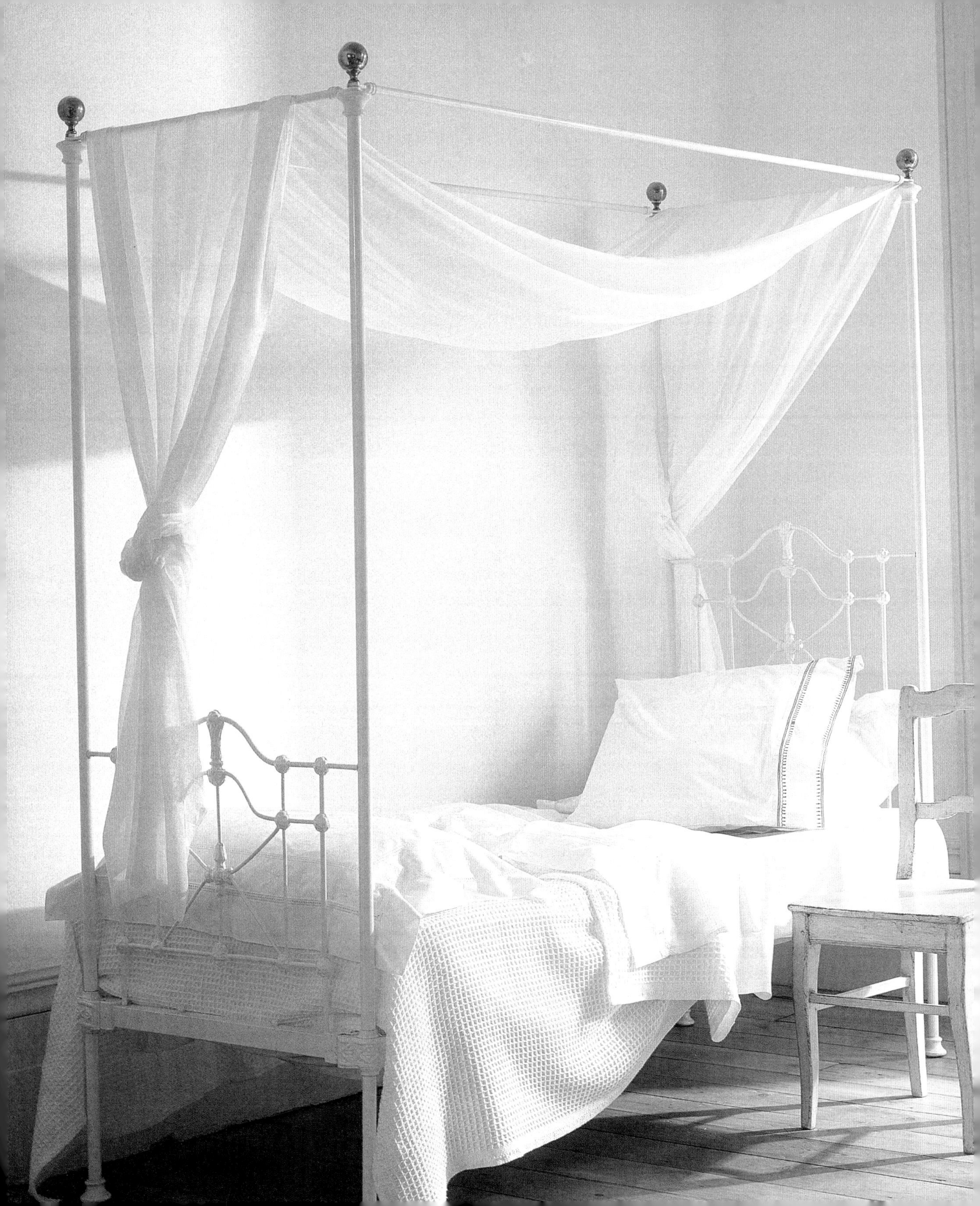

Sleep

Sleep is a great restorer. As we sleep, growth and repair hormones are released, regenerating skin cells, and as the activity-hormones switch off we relax all the muscles in the body and face. Sleep refreshes, builds up new energy supplies, renews blood, brain and body tissues, dispels stress and anxiety, heals aching limbs and soothes the mind. Dreaming is nature's way of rebalancing by discharging mental baggage, of sorting and organising memory and cognition at subconscious levels. It may be the most creative thing our minds ever do. Dreams can free our subconscious of its restraints, liberating creative energy which, if we can harness it by understanding the symbols and messages in our dreaming, can be immensely therapeutic.

Finding (or making) space for soul time is essential for balance and wholeness, even if it is just reading a few lines of inspirational work such as Thomas à Kempis or Lao-Tsu before you fall asleep (I keep several books of this kind by my bed).

We spend one-third of our lives asleep, and when deprived for long periods develop irritability, diminished cognitive function and eventually - in extremis - psychotic symptoms. Sleep is essential, and it is also integrating: how often do you 'sleep on a problem' and wake up with a solution?

Power-napping during the day, even if only for ten minutes is recognised as highly beneficial. I regard my cat with awe verging on envy as she snoozes the day away in between bursts of manic activity. Build a cat-nap into your day, and you'll find how deeply refreshing it is. It works wonders and clears your mind for a demanding afternoon.

HOW TO AVOID INSOMNIA

Fighting fatigue diverts the blood supply to the major organs leaving us pale and highlighting dark circles around the eyes. Sleep deprivation impairs immune function and can severly reduce mental clarity. So if you have problems sleeping well, try some of these remedies.

- **Establish a routine before bedtime: take half an hour to wind down, either by reading, meditation, some yoga stretches or a soak in a warm bath with essential oils (see page 174)**
- **Don't go to bed hungry**
- **Create a regular time-pattern: whatever time you go to bed, always get up at the same time in the morning**
- **If you are having a bad night's sleep, don't worry about it: maybe you don't need as much sleep as you think. Instead of tossing and turning and fretting, enjoy being warm and comfortable in bed, and concentrate on resting your body, relaxing from the head through to the toes**
- **If you've had a rotten night's sleep, don't be tempted to sleep deeply during the day (a cat-nap is fine), but rather do a yoga practice or meditate (see page 199)**
- **Don't go to bed with a quarrel or resentment on your mind: resolve it – or plan to – first**
- **Don't do demanding mental work just before bedtime**

Another delightful way of using essential oils is to put a few drops on to your pillow: rose or jasmine are luxurious, lavender calming, and ylang-ylang intoxicatingly aphrodisiac as well as sedative.

NATURAL WAYS TO GET TO SLEEP

- **Reduce the amounts of caffeine in your diet (tea, coffee, cola, chocolate)**
- **Open the window in the bedroom: a stuffy room can keep you awake**
- **Take at least half an hour of exercise in the fresh air during the day**
- **Don't drink a lot of alcohol, and never use it to get you to sleep: you'll end up with a restless night**
- **Feng-shui your bedroom**
- **Make love: sex is a great aid to sleep**
- **Don't go to bed hungry: have a malted drink or eat a lettuce sandwich – starch contains the essential amino acid trytophan which is a precursor of serotonin, and the milky sap of lettuce is deeply soporific**
- **If your mind is churning, do the mindful breathing exercise (see page 200)**
- **Drink a herb tea half an hour before you retire: balm, chamomile, and lime blossom (linden) teas are all soothing and relaxing**
- **Honey is a well-established nightcap: drink it in warm milk, or with lemon and hot water**
- **Herbal remedies such as valerian, kava and passiflora give you a restful night's sleep**
- **Make a pillow of dried hops, or of lavender: both scents are conducive to deep sleep**
- **Get stuck into a good novel for a while before you turn out the light, and allow your mind to stay with its story as you prepare for sleep, and it will carry you into unconsciousness**
- **Audio books are an excellent relaxant (unless they are really gripping), easing your mind away from the day's events and gently talking you to sleep**

ESSENTIAL OILS FOR SLEEP

The appropriate essential oils, either in a bath or burning in a fragrancer in the bedroom, can restore a broken sleep pattern and give you a restful night. Certain essential oils have powerfully soporific and soothing effects, and have been shown to lower the heart rate and deepen respiration.

Any of the following oils have a sedative effect, and can be used in combination – two or three maximum, 10-12 drops floating on the bath water, 3-4 drops in the burner.

Chamomile, lavender, melissa, neroli, patchouli, rose, sandalwood, ylang-ylang are all relaxing oils. Frankincense is warming and relaxing and promotes tranquillity, and marjoram has excellent soporific qualities.

Meditation

There are several techniques to calm the body, still the mind and bring you to a state of inner harmony and heightened awareness, inherited from Hinduism, Buddhism and Christianity. Some use the breathing, some objects of concentration, others use mantras. Whichever method you use, they all aim to bring the body and mind to a state of peace and wholeness. Following the breath brings the mind from its customary circling and wandering, and quietly restores us to that tranquillity and peace which leads to clarity and insight.

Meditation is a little drop of perfume that suffuses the day with its grace.
R. D. LAING

MINDFULNESS MEDITATION

The practice of following the breath is a simple way of quietening the mind, of stopping. It is about simple attention and awareness, not about achieving or 'doing'.

It has important health implications. Regular meditation has been shown to have thoroughly beneficial effects on both physical and phychological problems. Studies have been carried out by Dr. Jon Kabat-Zinn at Massachusetts Medical Center in the USA where over the years he has offered 'mindfulness meditation' sessions in stress-reduction clinics to sick patients with highly beneficial results in terms of both pain relief and recovery. Patients with anxiety disorders, cancers including breast and prostate, cardiac disease, hypertension, gastro-intestinal problems, chronic pain and psoriasis showed both short and long-term reduction in physical and psychological problems after a period of practising mindfulness meditation regularly. It keeps you youthful, too: the International Journal of Neuroscience showed that a group of fifty years-olds who had been meditating for five years were twelve years younger in health terms than a similar group of non-meditators. During the practice the blood flow to the brain is increased by 25 per cent!

MEDITATION IS GOOD FOR YOU

Meditation actually helps redress imbalances in the brain. In this state of deep relaxation EEG readings show that the left side of the brain (see page 77) becomes less active and the right side more so, enhancing intuitive and creative functions. It has been shown that meditation evokes the 'relaxation response', the opposite to the 'stress response' (see page 69) alpha waves increase, oxygen consumption and metabolic rate decrease, blood pressure drops, heart rate slows and muscles relax. In this rebalancing process the body normalises and immune function improves – to the extent that even orthodox medical practitioners are beginning to consider a daily meditation practice of considerable importance for anyone wishing to maintain a healthy lifestyle. Zen Buddhism is accepted as an effective complementary therapy.

'Your life is the creation of your mind' said the Buddha. In meditation you experience the essential nature of mind, its expansive, universal sky-like nature, and the fullness of being beyond patterns and habits. You glimpse your true inner nature, a fleeting vision of wholeness beyond the fragmentation of the distractions and craving, grasping inclinations of your mind.

A simple mindfulness meditation

Perhaps the best times of day to do a sitting practice of meditation are early morning to awaken the mind serenely and bring you to wholeness at the start of the day, and some time in the evening, to relax the body and quieten the mind before sleep but not just after eating since you are likely to become drowsy. Choose a quiet, private place in the house where you will not be disturbed by people or by the phone, a room that is warm and clean, with gentle lighting.

The essence of this practice is simplicity. Breath is the tool. It is a focusing practice that you can do in the car, on the bus, on a busy train or crowded tube, after a row with the boss, walking or even just washing up.

Meditation unties the knots in your mind and helps you stop so that your mind becomes calm and clear, like water after the mud has settled. It is a powerful practice that brings equanimity and insight when practised regularly.

MINDFUL BREATHING

Sit comfortably in as grounded a posture as possible (see pages 116-118). Close your eyes and start to consciously relax your face, your body and your breathing, focusing on the abdomen with its little rise and fall on the in and the out breath. As you exhale, release tension in the body, as you inhale, become tall: think of pushing the sky with your head, the earth with your knees (or feet if you are sitting in a chair). Release, relax, and rest in that peaceful space until you feel a balance of quietness and alertness.

If the everyday 'monkey-mind' is still whizzing around, use imagery to help it quieten. Think of yourself as a pebble sinking into the clear water of a lake. See it dropping slowly towards the lake bed until it comes to rest, leaving the surface of the water clear. Rest with the pebble at the bottom of the lake.

Once you are calm, bring your attention, your mindfulness, to your breath: simply breathe in, breathe out, remaining fully conscious of the process of breathing. You can mentally say 'I am breathing in', 'I am breathing out', or just 'in' and 'out'. It may take some practice before you are able to remain completely focused on the breathing and to stop your mind from wandering off to think about the shopping list or the new decor for the living room.

To keep the attention on the breath, you can continue by using the series of words below to guide you through your meditation, spending perhaps several minutes on each pair.

BREATHING IN:	BREATHING OUT:
'In'	'Out'
'Deep'	'Slow'
'Calm'	'Ease'
'Smile'	'Release'
'Space'	'Free'
'Present moment'	'Wonderful moment'

You can do this meditation with your eyes open but soft, with the 'limitless gaze' of peripheral vision, although many people find it easier to start with the eyes closed. The danger with closed eyes is that you wander into the labyrinth of the mind, or fall into a doze.

When your meditation is finished (don't time it, that creates a tension – it's over when it's over) stretch gently and sit for a minute or two to readjust before leaving the room.

DIFFICULTIES WITH MEDITATION

There are days when meditation works better than others, and in spite of its simplicity there are pitfalls. The mind is a clever trickster and rarely obedient to our wish to become quiet. So learn to watch your thoughts, to stand back and be detached from them, watch them like a movie but without becoming entangled and reacting to them. Labelling thoughts and distractions can be useful, recognising them as 'mind-waves', and feelings as 'emotion waves'. Let them go on their way. The less attached to them you learn to become, the more you experience inner stillness. If you are appalled at how your thoughts are running riot, be reassured: it may well mean that you have become quieter and simply are becoming aware of how noisy your thoughts habitually are!

Even if you are battling with a difficult life situation, simply holding it in awareness during meditation will do much to soothe and to give perspective, insight and awareness, and to offer peace amid the tumult. You can imagine your life, your thoughts, your problems as a waterfall, and that you are sitting behind it in the rocks. You can see them and hear them rushing past but you are not carried away by them.

REGULAR PRACTICE

Other common pitfalls when you first begin meditation are torpor and restlessness: you feel tired, heavy of body and dull of mind or are unable to sit still. These are natural problems and with regular practice, the mind will understand that it can relax without falling asleep, that it can be calm and alert at the same time and that you can breathe your body into stillness.

You may have doubts about meditation because you feel it isn't working. But don't worry: at some level, it will be. You don't do meditation, you let it happen. Remember that you are not trying to get somewhere or go anywhere. 'To meditate is not to achieve, but to be', in the words of the Zen Buddhist master Thich Nhat Hanh (see *Bookshelf* page 204.) The progress is the process itself. It is about being not doing. Regular attentive practice will bear fruit, so remember that doubting is natural and human.

OUT AND ABOUT

You can practice mindful breathing anywhere, any time, any circumstance. Walking in the fresh air, measure your breath with your footsteps. For instance, for every in-breath take three steps, for every out-breath take three steps. If you are moving very briskly it may be four steps. Stay focused on your footsteps in time with the breathing and become absorbed in the process of walking meditation. Walking down a street, become aware of your breathing. You will find this experience amazing: it brings the experience into full consciousness, and you will remember faces and places like vivid photographs in your head.

Much of the tension of travelling dissolves if you practise this. Travelling home from work on a busy train, breathe in and breathe out as you bring yourself back home into the present moment.

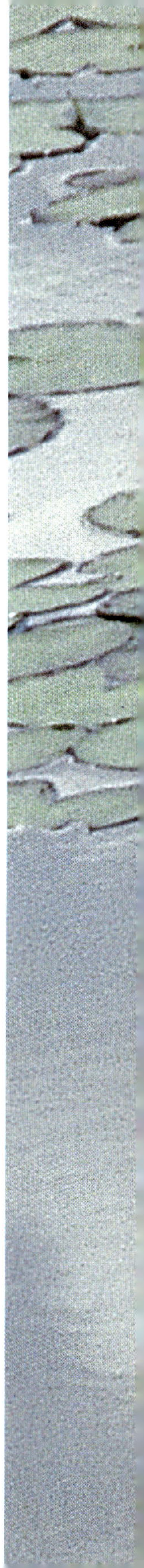

Do you think you can take over
the universe and improve it?
I do not believe it can be done.
The universe is sacred.
You cannot improve it.
If you try to change it,
you will ruin it.
If you try to hold it, you will lose it.

So sometimes things are ahead
and sometimes they are behind;
Sometimes breathing is hard
and sometimes it comes easily
Sometimes there is strength
and sometimes weakness;
Sometimes one is up
and sometimes down.

Therefore the sage avoids extremes,
excesses, and complacency.

LAO TSU
TAO TE CHING

If meditation brings you into the present moment, it cannot by definition distance you from immediate reality. The great tradition of mindfulness meditation is one that brings you closer to the richness of the everyday, it is not isolating and detached but rather verifies the mystic experience of the interconnectedness of everything.

Bookshelf

The Aesthetics of Music
ROGER SCRUTON, *OUP 1997*

Awakening the Spine
VANDA SCARAVELLI,
Harper Collins 1991

The Beauty Myth
NAOMI WOLF, *Vintage 1991*

Big Sur and the Oranges of Hieronymus Bosch
HENRY MILLER,
Flamingo 1993

Biorhythms
PETER WEST, *Elements 1999*

Body Learning MICHAEL GELB, *Aurum Press 1981*

The Book of Yoga
SIVANANDA YOGA CENTRE,
Ebury 1983

Emotional Intelligence
DANIEL GOLEMAN,
Bloomsbury 1996

Ending the Mother War
JAYNE BUXTON,
Macmillan 1998

Fitness and Health
BRIAN J. STARKEY,
Human Kinetics 1990

Food Combining for Health DORIS GRANT AND JEAN JOICE,
Thorsons 1984

Foods for Mind and Body
MICHAEL VAN STRATEN,
Harper Collins 1997

The Good Life
Demos Collection 1998

The Human Brain
SUSAN GREENFIELD,
Weidenfeld and Nicolson 1997

Light on Yoga
BKS IYENGAR,
Unwin 1984

A Little Book of Women Mystics
CAROL LEE FLANDERS,
Harper Collins 1995

Love Life
DR. JANET RIBSTEIN,
Fourth Estate 1997

The Mind Miracle DR. D.S. KHALSA, *Arrow 1998*

The Miracle of Mindfulness, Being Peace, Touching Peace and other titles by THICH NHAT HANH,
Rider Books

New Green Pharmacy
BARBARA GRIGGS
Vermilion 1997

The Organic Directory
Green Earth Books 1997

The Perennial Philosophy
ALDOUS HUXLEY,
Harper Colophon 1970

Stress Busters ROBERT HOLDEN, *Thorsons 1992*

Where to Buy Organic Food
Soil Association 1998

The Sickening Mind
PAUL MARTIN,
Harper Collins 1997

Solitude ANTHONY STORR,
Flamingo 1989

Six Memos for a New Millennium
ITALO CALVINO,
Jonathan Cape 1992

A Time to Keep Silence
PATRICK LEIGH FERMOR,
John Murray 1982

The Wit and Wisdom of Oscar Wilde ED. ALVIN REDMAN, *Dover NY 1952*

Useful addresses

Alexander Technique International
0171 281 7639

Association for Research into the Science of Enjoyment (ARISE)
PO Box 11446 London
SW18 5ZH
0181 874 5548

Auro organic paints
01799 584042

British Association for Behavioural and Cognitive Psychotherapies
BABCP
PO Box 9, Accrington,
BB5 2GD

Community Of Interbeing
(Thich Nhat Hanh)
Plum Village,
Meyrac,
47120 Loubes-Bernac,
France

Council for Complementary and Alternative medicine,
Suite D,
Park House,
206-8 Latimer Road,
London W10 6RE
0181 968 3862

Eco-balls (laundry)
Birchwood House
Briar Lane
Croydon
Surry CR0 5AD

Eco-Info Helpline
01225 442288

Ecover products
01635 528240

The Energy Saving Trust
0345 277200

Fragrant Earth
(essential oils, Fuller's Earth)
01458 831216

Friends of the Earth
0171 490 1555

The Henry Doubleday Research Association,
Ryton Organic Gardens,
Coventry CV83LG

National Institute of Medical Herbalists
01392 426 022

Natural Collection
(house decor)
01225 44228

Natural Paints
01539 732866

Paperback
(recycled paper and office supplies)
0181 980 5580

The Soil Association
0117 929 0661

Stress Management Training
(tapes, courses, groups, self-help)
01983 868166

Index

Photo acknowledgements

All photographs by Michelle Garrett except as credited below.

8-9 Tom Leighton/Homes & Gardens © IPC, Robert Harding Syndication; 10 Tom Leighton/Homes & Gardens © IPC, Robert Harding Syndication; 11 Polly Wreford/Homes & Ideas, © IPC, Robert Harding Syndication; 12 James Merrill/Homes & Gardens © IPC, Robert Harding Syndication; 16 Lucinda Symons/Inspirations © GE Magazines Ltd; 17 Sandra Lane/Woman & Home © IPC, Robert Harding Syndication; 18 Simon Upton/Homes & Gardens © IPC, Robert Harding Syndication; 19 Ian Skelton/Homes & Ideas © IPC, Robert Harding Syndication; 21 Tom Leighton/Homes & Gardens © IPC, Robert Harding Syndication; 24 Polly Wreford/Homes & Ideas © IPC, Robert Harding Syndication; 25 Polly Wreford/Homes & Gardens © IPC, Robert Harding Syndication; 27 Nick Pope/Options © IPC, Robert Harding Syndication; 28-29 Tom Leighton/Homes & Gardens © IPC, Robert Harding Syndication; 30 Grey Zisser/Options © IPC, Robert Harding Syndication; 31 Simon Harris/Robert Harding Picture Library; 35 Robert Harding Picture Library; 37 Jan Baldwin/Homes & Gardens © IPC, Robert Harding Syndication; 38 Elizabeth Zeschin/Homes & Gardens © IPC, Robert Harding Syndication; 39 Mann & Mann/Options © IPC, Robert Harding Syndication; 46 Pia Tryde/Options © IPC, Robert Harding Syndication; 48-49 Anna Hodgson/Homes & Gardens © IPC, Robert Harding Syndication; 53 Elizabeth Zeschin/Homes & Gardens © IPC, Robert Harding Syndication; 73 Sandra Lane/Homes & Gardens © IPC, Robert Harding Syndication; 84 Chris Drake/Options © IPC, Robert Harding Syndication; 85 David Oldfield/Options © IPC, Robert Harding Syndication; 127 Michelle Garrett/Options © IPC, Robert Harding Syndication; 166-167 Debi Treloar/Inspirations © GE Magazine, Robert Harding Syndication; 171 John Mason/Homes & Gardens © IPC, Robert Harding Syndication; 196 Elizabeth Zeschin/Homes & Gardens © IPC, Robert Harding Syndication; 198 John Mason/Homes & Gardens © IPC, Robert Harding Syndication.